Peter Hennessy

Historian

'An absorbing and intriguing

John Simpson

World Affairs Editor, BBC News

'Five generations of Jonathan Lawley's family have known and served in the Andaman Islands. Now, the Indian authorities have built an illegal road for tourists to gawp at the Jarawa, who wear no clothes and use bows and arrows to hunt. Jonathan Lawley's account of what has happened is deeply moving and deserves our attention and our support.'

Matthew Parris

Writer and Broadcaster

'A book of anthropological importance, with a message pivotal to the survival of an indigenous island society on the edge of extinction, written with invaluable insight from the author's own family history in connection with the islands. A fine balance of information and passion.'

Christopher Matthew

Writer and Broadcaster

'By turns astonishing and deeply troubling. Dr Lawley's book is truly a revelation.'

Richard Luce

Former UK Government Minister

'Jonathan Lawley is ideally qualified to tell the story of the Jawara tribe. His long family history in India and the Andamans, plus his own distinguished service as an Administrator in southern Africa, enables him to describe with realistic empathy the tribe's wish to continue its unique way of life without disturbance from the rest of us. For anyone interested in the remarkable diversity of our planet, reading *A Road to Extinction* is a must. It is a fascinating book and I strongly recommend it.'

Hugh Tyndale-Biscoe

Former Chief Research Scientist, CSIRO

'In this new book Jonathan Lawley has turned his attention to the colonial service of his own family in India and the Andaman Islands, tracing the story of the islands and their aboriginal inhabitants through to the present day. It is a fascinating but sombre tale.'

John Smith
Colonial Historian
'A gripping mix of history, memoir and polemic about a people who have managed to avoid all that has happened to most of humanity over the last 60,000 years. Dr Lawley pleads powerfully that their wishes to remain apart be respected and makes it clear that if they are not, contact with our civilization will kill them.'

Michael Holman
Former Africa Editor, The Financial Times
'A compelling appeal for the world to wake up and save this last redoubt of a world that otherwise faces imminent extinction.'

Michael Dawe
International consultant
'A superb read in which Jonathan Lawley presents the case for cultural separateness as beautifully as the archive stories of his family. Most of my professional life, I and others in Third World workforce development have tried to include people in 'international rules-based systems'. It therefore turns things on their head to argue that Andamanese tribes should be left alone.

This is different from apartheid. In this case, it is the tribes that have asked to be left alone, so the thrust of the argument is clear—and cultures should either be wholly in the international system or wholly outside it; a halfway point is just damaging to the weaker group, especially where cultures are beguiled into joining the international system by promises that are never delivered. (If they knew the reality—or had better instincts— perhaps they too would adopt the strategy that the Jarawa have adopted and which we find so perplexing.)

Knowing India's development model from the inside I struggle to be optimistic about the destructive Andaman Trunk Road that Jonathan Lawley writes about, and I doubt India's Prime Minister Narendra Modi is very worried about a group of stone-age hunter-gatherers who don't vote—but I sincerely hope I am wrong.

If the Andaman Islands had greater military value, India would probably have taken greater steps to keep the islands and their people more isolated. Instead tourism beckons, and cultural devastation.

This book needs to be read widely—and acted upon.'

Author's foreword

A Road to Extinction is a plea for the survival of a group of palaeolithic tribespeople who, against the odds, have managed to retain their extraordinary culture in the forests of the Andaman Islands, 400 miles off the coast of Burma in the Indian Ocean. The Andamans were taken over by the British in the late 1850s and my family was involved for several years in their administration. They now belong to India.

There are passionate arguments about the British during the days of the Raj, especially in the case of the Andamans, the primary purpose of which, for the British, was the building of a penal colony that would remove from mainland India those convicted of crimes during the Mutiny of 1857.

I acknowledge that my own view of the Raj is more benign than that of most contemporary writers, especially Indian historians and those whose subjects are imperialism, Indian nationalism and human rights.

I am quite prepared to defend my own position on the British, who I think are too often misrepresented, but to rake over the past on this occasion is to miss the point, even if there is a case for saying that the ills of the islanders are part of Britain's colonial legacy.

The point that now needs to be addressed is that a group of islanders, whose origins can be traced back 100,000 years and who have resisted all efforts to accommodate them into modern civilization, are at risk of extinction and that there is currently no meaningful plan to protect their interests, other than by doing exactly what they do not want and engaging them in development programmes and giving them handouts.

Irrespective of what mistakes the British may have made in the past, India has had exclusive responsibility for these tribespeople for nearly 70 years and during this time its involvement has been a complete and destructive failure. India needs to recognise the urgency of the situation and intercede, at last, to give the people the security but also the privacy that they require, encouraged if necessary by other sovereign states.

That is what this book is all about. If readings of it divert instead into a debate about the rights and wrongs of British rule a century ago, or into the nature of imperialism, especially in order to exonerate India and the current government of the Andaman and Nicobar Islands, or even into the language that I use and have grown up with, which is obviously and understandably different from the language used by anthropologists today, that would not only be an act of self-righteous evasion, it would be to pile one moral outrage on another.

Jonathan Lawley was born in India and educated in Southern Africa and Cambridge. He joined the Colonial Service in Northern Rhodesia, became fluent in the Tonga language of the Zambezi Valley and was the last British District Commissioner in independent Zambia. Fluency in French took him to the Congo, Morocco and Mauritius. His interest in management development led him to set up and run a Rio Tinto-funded programme to develop the first indigenous technical managers for the mining industry in Southern Africa, a field of expertise in which he went on to take a PhD. After retirement he became Africa Director of British Executive Service Overseas (BESO), was the first Director of the Royal African Society and is now adviser to the Business Council for Africa.

Previous publications
Transcending culture: Developing Africa's technical managers
Beyond the Malachite Hills
Zambia since 1960

A ROAD TO EXTINCTION

TO MY MOTHER

WHO ALWAYS UNDERSTOOD WHY THE
ANDAMANS ARE SO SPECIAL

JONATHAN LAWLEY

A ROAD TO EXTINCTION

CAN PALEOLITHIC AFRICANS SURVIVE IN THE ANDAMAN ISLANDS?

EDITED BY STEPHEN GAMES

Published 2020 in Great Britain by
EnvelopeBooks
A New Premises venture

EnvelopeBooks
12 Wellfield Avenue
London N10 2EA

Cover design
by Booklaunch

A CIP catalogue record for this title is available from the
British Library

ISBN 9781838172015

Designed by Booklaunch
www.envelopebooks.co.uk

Contents

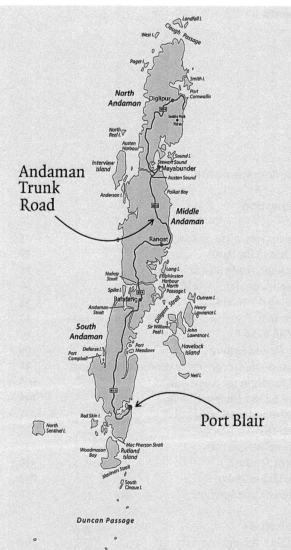

Landfall I.

Cleugh Passage

West I.

Paget I.

Smith I.

North Andaman

Diglipur

Port Cornwallis

NH4

Saddle Peak
732 m.

North Reef I.

Austen Harbour

Sound I.

Stewart Sound

Interview Island

Mayabunder

Austen Sound

Anderson I.

Paikat Bay

NH4

Middle Andaman

Rangat

Long I.

Elphinston Harbour

Hofray Strait

North Passage I.

Spike I.

NH4

Outram I.

Baratang

Henry Lawrence I.

Andaman Strait

Diligent Strait

South Andaman

Sir William Peel I.

John Lawrence I.

Defense I.

Port Campbell

Port Meadows

Havelock Island

Neil I.

NH4

Andaman Trunk Road

Port Blair

Red Skin I.

North Sentinel I.

Mac Pherson Strait

Woodmason Bay

Rutland Island

Manners Strait

South Cinque I.

Duncan Passage

Little Andaman

West Bay

Hut Bay

South Bay

THE ANDAMAN ISLANDS

Acknowledgements

It was Michael Holman, former Africa Editor of the *Financial Times* and fellow African, who reinforced my realization that there was more to my links with the Andamans than just a family memoir from the days of the Raj. I could not have done without his understanding of what is at issue and his encouragement that I write it down. I have likewise been encouraged by writers and broadcasters Christopher Matthew and Matthew Parris, for their professional perspectives on what started out as a very daunting project.

On the family side, top of the list comes my sister Veronica who has herself been to the Andamans and gave me vital contacts and advice. Nicky Coldstream gave me a lot of time and feedback on an early draft. First cousins Tim Deane and Iain Lowis and Tim's son Jamie provided photographs as well as support.

I owe a huge debt of gratitude to Terry Anne Barringer, scholar and librarian specialising in all matters related to the British Empire and Commonwealth and Colonial Service. Former Brigadier Hugh Willing, regimental historian who speaks Swahili, Arabic and Gurkhali and knows the Andamans, enlightened me on the military encounters there that led to the award of an unprecedented number of Victoria crosses. Also on the military side I was helped by my friend and neighbour Barry Peek who introduced me to a book on British and Indian Army special operations during the Japanese occupation of the Andamans during the Second World War.

In May 2018 daughter Juliet and I paid a visit to the Andamans to follow up on Veronica's contacts. Although we were unable to meet Prof Francis Neelham and Rashida Iqbal, we received great help and well informed local perspectives from three members of the Local Born Society: Denis Giles, editor of the *Andaman Chronicle*, Mukeshwar Lall, director of the Kala Pani Museum, and John Lobo, who had memories of the Japanese occupation. Our loyal taxi driver Aziz also gave us the valuable viewpoint of a younger generation of settlers.

Back in the UK I wish to thank Lord (Peter) Hennessy, the writer and historian, and Lord (Richard) Luce, once a District Officer in Her Majesty's Overseas Civil Service, for their interest and support and wonderful endorsements. Hugely encouraging also has been the interest shown by Professor Vanessa Hayes of the Garvan Institute in Australia, an expert on the Bushmen or San people of Botswana and Namibia. The link between the Andamans and her new researches into the origins of mankind is discussed in the book.

Friends who have shown helpful interest include John Raison, who edited the first draft of the book, Jessamy Reynolds who was born in India, Michael Dawe for a professional's grasp of the main issue, Dorothy Casey, Stephanie Powell, and India Owen-Jones of Fauna and Flora International. I have also been encouraged by Professors Erika Hagelberg and Clare Anderson, both of whom know the Andamans well and share the growing swell of concern for the survival of the indigenous inhabitants.

I am lucky to have been in touch with Hugh, the son of my former headmaster Eric Tyndale-Biscoe whose influence on all of us, British and Indian, who had the good fortune to have been at his wonderfully conceived prep school in Kashmir in WW2, has been lifelong. Hugh, who knows India well, has provided valuable help and advice. Most encouraging too has been the interest shown by fellow former member of the Colonial Service John Smith and from another doyen, John Simpson, world affairs editor of BBC News, who is peerless in his depth of understanding of what is going on around the world and particularly in southern Africa

Most recent has been my association with Stephen Games, editor of *Booklaunch*, who has shown a quite incredible ability to understand and interpret where I am coming from and to whom I am particularly grateful for his insightful copy editing, fact checking and support.

Finally, but far from last, my most special thanks go to my wife Sarah who, due to illness, had to give up her place on our Andamans adventure but went on to type the entire manuscript of this book, parts of it several times over.

Jonathan Lawley
Aldeburgh, Suffolk
May 2020

Introduction

I come from a background of life and work in both pre- and post-independence Africa which I love, and before that from the positive influence of a happy Indian childhood. I am proud of the immensity of British achievements in the Commonwealth and scornful of the preconceived and mostly ill-informed idea that as a nation we have something to be ashamed of. Beyond that I feel that because of our experience and the way we are regarded, we have achieved more than we realize in helping the developing world to help itself.

The Andamans' story, however, does not fit into any historical stereotype. The British failed to understand or deal with hugely problematic issues there and so do the Indians who now control the islands.

The background to my special interest in these remote islands in the Bay of Bengal lies in a five-generation family link and a connection with India that goes back to the days of the East India Company. Most memorably my mother held me spellbound as a child in India with her tales of her own childhood on the islands, while my adult interest in the islands was reignited by my research for a book on our family's involvement with India. I read my late mother's memoir of her father, whose life and career culminated in his spending most of his last years in the Andamans acting as commissioner. I also read his two histories of the islands written after he had supervised the censuses of 1911 and 1921, and a collection of articles by my grandmother on life in the islands written more than a century ago for British and Indian periodicals.

All the while I found myself increasingly intrigued by accounts of a unique interaction between modern man and people who hated and feared civilization as represented by their British and then Indian occupiers.

The depth of my interest grew as I came to understand that the indigenous attitude to the outside world was fully justified; external contact up to the present day has led to the extinction of nine of the islands' original twelve tribes, for reasons that I will explore. Two of the tribes that survive relatively unaffected have had virtually no contact with outsiders. The third, of which a few still remain, has been reduced to a pitiful and humiliating state of dependency.

All that I have read, seen and heard has led me to fear for the future of these people. While most of us probably know nothing of them, I am convinced that the world would be immensely poorer for their disappearance. I have come to see that we have much to learn from them and much more than they need learn from us.

In many respects, such as the minimal impact their way of life has on the natural world, they are far above us. While modern man continues to destroy the environment through population growth, deforestation, global warming and species destruction, the Andamanese way of life is perfectly compatible with it.

Among other things, this is a conservation issue that involves our own species. I hope fervently that the world will wake up quickly to its importance and that this book will play some part in hastening the process.

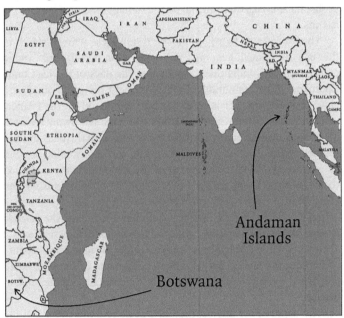

Chapter 1

The Andaman Trunk Road

How is it that a new road running through the pristine forests of the remote Andaman Islands threatens the oldest tribe of human beings in the whole world—people who for thousands of years had no contact with civilization, then rightly came to see it as threatening their culture, way of life and very existence?

The Andamans, with the Nicobar Islands, are one of eight territories or provinces administered by India. Whereas the Nicobarese, who originate from Asia and inhabit the southern islands, have always had trading relations with neighbouring countries, the Andamanese tribes—whose provenance until recently nobody knew—have always kept themselves to themselves.

Work on the Andaman Trunk Road (ATR) started in the 1970s without reference to the people. When workers started to be killed by members of the Jarawa tribe, construction was officially banned by the Indian Supreme Court but continued none the less. In 2002 the court ordered the closure of the new road but financial pressures kept it open. The disaster that the Jarawa had fought for centuries to prevent then started to unfold.

Prospects for the Jarawa have been in rapid decline since Indian independence in 1947 and the arrival of new settlers, particularly refugees from Bangladesh and Burma, as well as Indian ex-servicemen, to set up villages on what the Jarawa have always regarded as traditional tribal land.

Under British rule—apart from Port Blair, neighbouring settlements in the south of South Andaman, a small hospital at Kadamtala on Middle Andaman, and a few outposts and trading posts along the coasts—virtually the whole island chain was regarded as the domain of the aboriginal native tribes. Travel was uniformly by sea. My grandfather's travels when he was supervising the censuses of 1911 and 1921 were entirely by boat. Thus all contact with the tribes took place on the coast, not inland, and in accordance with British policy they were left to continue the age-old way of life they valued so much, leaving untouched the forest interior where they hunted wild pig and collected food and medicine.

Until the arrival of the settlers there was no need for a road. Besides, any pressure to build it could have been resisted by the local administrators had they thought about the likely effect on the Jarawa. The consequences of the road should have been obvious; unfortunately, no one gave any consideration to the tribes and their need above all to be left alone. Thus it was that, without significant opposition, construction went ahead. In the teeth of official Indian government policy, the local authorities tacitly welcomed the road and the settlers that it attracted. The Jarawa retaliated by killing construction workers and attacking settlements.

It was then that a Jarawa boy called Enmi broke his leg during a tribal raid and his treatment in hospital in Port Blair produced a degree of reconciliation, with the result that travel along the ATR suddenly became much safer. Incidents continued, however, with a visiting minister and a newly set-up police outpost being robbed at arrowpoint.

A new factor now arose, one destined to have more lasting consequences than anything else. It came from the wish among mainly local entrepreneurs—bus and taxi owners and hoteliers—to exploit the road for what some in the West might term 'eco-tourism'. It would be truer to say that there were massive profits to be made from exploiting the desire of tourists to see their strange, aboriginal neighbours. Suddenly, visitors started to arrive in large numbers from the Indian mainland.

My elder daughter Juliet and I got a perspective on the phenomenon when we flew into Port Blair in mid-2018. I am not sure quite what we expected; a quiet little island airport with small aircraft bringing in perhaps two or three dozen tourists a day. I was astounded by the reality. The airport was heaving with tourists: there were hundreds arriving and leaving each day. One morning we visited the great expanse in the middle of the city where long convoys of vehicles, their exhausts belching clouds of smoke, headed off in convoys for the ATR.

The vast majority of the tourists were middle-class Indians intrigued at the prospect of seeing naked stone-age people on Indian soil. The Andamans are now the most popular of all destinations for

Indian tourists, whose interest in historical sites like Ross Island and the Cellular Jail is limited. They crave encounters with humanity's prehistoric peoples.

Access to the ATR is via the new road south through the city, passing the airport and swinging north to the Jiratang Check Point on the edge of the Jarawa Reserve. There, travellers are greeted by huge notice boards setting out the Dos and Don'ts of driving along the ATR. These include the requirement for permits and driving only in convoy, and a ban on lifts and gifts for tribespeople and on photography.

The convoys with their police escorts start off along a narrow tarred road. Very soon they pass through thick jungle with huge trees. Tropical rainforest vegetation makes up a mostly unspoiled landscape all along the ATR. Beneath the trees, many in flower, is a virtually impenetrable tangle of ferns, creepers and young trees growing in the rich volcanic soil, all struggling upwards towards the light.

The terrain is undulating, descending to fast-flowing streams, and the road takes long sweeps round low hills. From the higher points emerge a scattering of particularly tall trees. The vegetation thins out as you approach larger crystal-clear, rushing water courses. Here and there, from higher points, dramatic views open up over the seemingly unbroken canopy but mostly the dense tree cover hems us in. It is only when the long road skirts the east coast of South Andaman that the views suddenly become spectacular and reveal a watery vista towards Havelock and neighboring islands across the sea.

Turning inland again, the road reaches villages flanked by coconut, betel and areca plantations which intrude on the mass of the forest. In the early days of the road, there was always the danger of Jarawa attacks. Now things are calmer, travelers along the ATR are more likely to see Jarawa women and children beside the road.

There is still a remote possibility that travelers can watch distant groups of Jarawa engaged in age-old activities such as gathering the jungle fruits and roots that make up their traditional diet. They may even see parties of men hunting wild boar or women collecting honey. Such sightings are highly prized.

By contrast the women and children beside the road have their hands out and seem to be begging, and buses stop illegally so that the tourists can take photographs of them and hand out gifts, particularly packets of biscuits, but also torches, boxes of matches, clothing, and pots and pans. Sometimes tourists barter biscuits for honey or crabmeat, or a local bow and arrow or spear. The exchanges are invariably exploitative and unequal.

More and more the Jarawa are becoming used to handouts and dependent on them. This affects their diet, puts their good health at risk, and creates new tastes and expectations. Vehicles that do not stop are sometimes chased. A journalist wrote recently of the sad sight of women and children running alongside the road with arms outstretched shouting '*do, do, do*' in Hindi, meaning 'give, give, give'.

Some in the Jarawa population see clearly what is happening to their tribe and seek to reverse the damage. The people of the Tirrur area are particularly keen to see a return to traditional behaviour because the encroachment of tourists and settler villages is affecting the Jarawa's equilibrium, as well as altering and damaging people's perceptions of them. There have also been cases of sexual exploitation including prostitution and the filming of naked women and children performing dances in exchange for gifts. In at least one case this happened with the connivance of the policeman who was supposed to be protecting them.

Critics of the government point to the failure to prosecute settlers whose poaching of wild boar has degraded the environment and more than anything else infuriates the Jarawa. Poaching attracts even stronger opposition than the incursions of traffickers of alcohol and drugs. There is also talk now of building a railway.

I was moved recently by the quiet voices of two young Jarawa men interviewed for an internet broadcast. It was one of the first times that anyone from the tribe had spoken out. Until now their concerns had gone unrepresented because they preferred to avoid contact and were regarded as voiceless.

The two representatives spoke calmly and without emotion to the French journalist interviewing them. He had gained access to the Jarawa reserve via the ATR; had he broken in on them a few years earlier he might not have emerged from the jungle alive. The tribesmen spoke in their own language, saying that all they had seen of civilization was bad. They said the Jarawa had never been consulted about anything and added that they did not know what was going on or what to do about the future. Their traditional life gave them everything they needed and wanted, which was peace, happiness and the absence of worry. They hated noise. Mainly they just wanted to be left alone.

Only the Indian Government has the power to save the Jarawa on behalf of mankind. But can it be persuaded and has it got the will?

Chapter 2
Back to the Past

North Sentinel is the most westerly of the Andaman Islands in an archipelago with which my family has connections going back to the 1880s. All my life I had dreamt of seeing this remote, unspoilt and almost hallowed place where my mother was brought up and where my grandfather had been deputy commissioner in the days of the British Raj. The islands had become part of the Indian Empire in 1857 when a penal colony was established there because of the shortage of accommodation in Indian jails to house those arrested after taking part in the Indian Mutiny of that year.

The Andamans today are an Indian dependency closer to Burma (Myanmar) than to mainland India and had featured in my imagination since early childhood, when my mother used to tell me tales of living in large houses surrounded by wide lawns set in forested islands surrounded by coral reefs. There were long views across the bay of other islands and her parents would take her and her sisters and brother to visit communities of friendly islanders there, where they would exchange loving hugs with little black people who wore no clothes and hunted with bows and arrows.

Besides the Andamans connection I had boyhood memories of pre-independence India—an India that had had a deep and lifelong influence on the way I saw the world. Until independence I had taken India for granted and been made blissfully happy there, until it was suddenly taken from me at the age of eleven, severing the contentment of my early years. Now I was opening a door that had been closed since 1947.

I had had no desire to return to India before. My childhood memories were so strong and so happy, I did not want to spoil them. At a smart English prep school that seemed to stand for nothing, I was unhappy. I suffered a sort of lonely bereavement there and with

Port Blair and Ross Island in the 1870s. Bottom right: The Governor's residence.

my parents now resettled in Africa, there was nobody who could begin to understand or share my feelings.

My childhood on the North West Frontier had been free and adventurous. I had had lots of contact with the locals including the boys in the bazaars, and I spoke Hindustani fluently. For two years I had been at a wonderful boarding school in Kashmir where the motto was, 'In All Things Be Men', and the emphasis was on the way we lived our lives and the development of character, including the values and strengths, moral and physical, to help us help others.

Above: The author, 1930s. Below: Boarding school in Kashmir on V.E. Day, 1945.

Respect for fellows down to the poorest coolie was fundamental. So we climbed to great heights and camped in the surrounding mountains, swam miles in limpid lakes, and paddled *shikaras* in races and played hockey barefoot against local schools.

Amazing as it may seem nowadays, we all bought into the philosophy. It was the open attitude to race that for me had a life-long influence and that came into play with greatest impact after I joined my family in southern Africa. I was shocked by the white racism I found there and its seemingly total disregard for the dignity of the Blacks. Even at the age of twelve I regarded it as suicidal. The difference in the mutual respect I had lived with and seen prevail in India was fundamental in leading me into a career in Her Majesty's Overseas Civil Service, the approach to which I saw as essential for the future of southern Africa. I felt the service would be a role model for a misguided South Africa that I became convinced would respond to British ideals. After all, the country had loyally supported us after the Boer War and was our ally in two world wars.

Beyond my mother's stories and influence, my interest in the long family involvement with the Andaman islands was fuelled by several factors including a recent visit by my sister Veronica, by my mother's memoir of her father, and by a collection of articles by grandmother Bessie on Andaman life that my mother had passed on to me before she died. They were all written more than a hundred years ago and most had been published in British and Indian journals and newspapers. Later I began to appreciate the importance to the islands of my grandfather's work, which I gained a better understanding of after reading the two books he had written after the censuses he supervised in 1911 and 1921.

Following the original British occupation of the Andaman islands there was a fall of almost biblical proportions in the population of indigenous Andamanese. At first this had gone unnoticed due to the almost total lack of contact with the British on the islands. The effect, however, was devastating. The number of tribes shrank from its original twelve to only three. The tribes that have remained are those that have been best at keeping outsiders at a distance.

Of these, the Onge were responsible for murdering the crew of the shipwrecked *Assam Valley* in 1867 but later came to be regarded as semi-friendly. They live on Little Andaman where there are many new settlers, and though they still exist in reasonable numbers have now been reduced to almost complete dependency and a sedentary state in which they do virtually nothing. Then there are Sentinelese whose numbers are small due to the size of their island but who remain viable and extremely hostile and are the subject of a later chapter. Only the Jarawa on South Andaman remain in reasonable numbers, thanks to their avoidance of contact but who are now threatened, as described in Chapter 1, by the arrival of settlers, by the opening up of the Andaman Trunk Road (the ATR) and by the incursions of tourists.

Visiting Port Blair was a way of reaching my wonderful, deeply sensitive mother. Her instincts, it seemed to me, were that the future of the Andaman islands and their inhabitants were important, and I think she hoped that I would come to feel the same way. She also hoped that I would come to share her loyalty to her father, her love for him and her recognition of the significance of his achievements during his 22 years in the islands.

Chapter 3

What the World Stands to Lose

Since *homo sapiens* spread from Africa tens of thousands of years ago, contact between people of different backgrounds has allowed us to learn much from each other, giving rise to today's rich tapestry of knowledge. In all that time the Andamanese have bypassed these transactions of experience and held on only to what they had before. If that seems to us like a loss of opportunity, we should consider how much of what we knew before our new-found knowledge has over-shadowed.

In particular the whole area of instinct remains a vital part of the tribal psyche but ranks much lower for us. For us, nearly all knowledge is a good thing in itself. We assume that interchange of ideas between people is of educational value, and that contact will broaden and enlighten us and generally lead to beneficial new ways of seeing the world.

The Andamanese regard such a notion very differently. Instinct tells them to avoid contact with anything that could lead to change. They have made it abundantly clear that they do not want or feel they need anything that threatens a way of life they value above all else, and that they do not wish to associate with the rest of humanity.

Thus are our ways of seeing the world totally opposite, and those who want to teach the Andamanese to read and write, and to cultivate, plant crops and tend plantations, are bound to fail. These are not people whom we should try to change, no matter how caring we might feel towards them, or how gently we approach them. The dilemma for us is how to do the best for them—since we have far more agency and autonomy than they do—without our affecting them in any way that diverts them from their state of innocence.

So while our top priority must be saving the Jarawa and the Sentinelese from extinction, our next priority is how to understand them better, especially in respect of their thought processes. If we can better fathom how these earliest hunter-gatherer ancestors of ours think, we may be better able to help them in ways that will make sense to them within their own set of values.

The Andamanese tribes are not a 'backward' people, any more than are those from the more remote parts of Papua New Guinea and the Amazon rain forest. But they are different, and the difference arises from the fact that due to an extraordinary set of circumstances, they appear to be largely unchanged from how they were tens of thousands of years ago.

Our understanding of the mysterious origins of the Andamanese is very recent and dates only from the 1990s. A sample of hair collected in 1908 by the father of modern social anthropology, Alfred Radcliffe-Brown, was discovered in Cambridge in an old glass cabinet by a British bio-scientist, Erika Hagelberg. Her study of its DNA revealed that the Andamanese tribes must have arrived from Africa around 60,000 years ago—long before what is now the Bay of Bengal, a volcanic area, was flooded by the sea and well before the earliest global navigators. For many thousands of years the Andamanese were left undisturbed to continue the same hunter-gatherer existence they had known in African, and in similar climatic conditions.

Since the 1990s, a survey carried out by Professor Vanessa Hayes of the Garvan Institute in Australia has suggested very specifically that our earliest ancestors came from great wetlands in what is now Botswana, part of which is the Okavango Delta and the neighbouring great dried-up Makgadikgadi plains. It is a part of the world I know well.

So our earliest ancestors are the Bushmen or San people. It seems to me both wonderful and extraordinary that a few of their direct descendants, people who retain their way of life and outlook, still exist in the Andaman Islands. What is terrible is that they are totally vulnerable, powerless and voiceless, and that they lack an understanding of exactly how they are threatened—though maybe they would accuse us of exactly the same.

There are basic things that we have lost over the millennia or failed to remember that they could teach us. One small example is our loss of basic instinct and our unawareness of the forces of nature. In 2004 they sensed the approaching tsunami and moved to higher ground. That instinct saved their lives. There were no deaths among them but hundreds of settlers were drowned. More broadly, they have an instinctive fear of the danger of civilization's temptations—something they have continued to oppose at every turn—compared with our almost suicidal embrace of the new. For them, the rejection of civilization is long-standing. Instinct has prepared them to go to any lengths to protect it. They are right to conclude that, unlike us, change would be their undoing.

Sadly, tourism has made them in to a human zoo, not least because they wear no clothes. But the Andamanese tribes are not mere savages to be gawped at. They are successful human beings with a successful way of life. For them the accumulation of wealth and possessions plays no part in their behaviour or in how an individual is seen by the rest of the community. Property is communal; when someone is asked for something that we might regard as their own, they are bound to hand it over. Theft, therefore, is virtually unknown. What matters most is kindness and hospitality. There are no laws or punishments for bad behaviour, only a downgrading of the individual's reputation and how they are seen by their peers. The custom and practice of giving an offender a smaller cut of a roast pig, for example, is punishment enough. There is universal respect for age and authority; wisdom is the province of older people. Most positive of all is the pursuit of happiness, which finds expression through frequent dancing.

Because they live in perfect balance with the environment, the Jarawa and the Sentinelese enjoy outstandingly good health. Their food and medicines are obtained from roots and fruits as well as honey to treat illness. Attitudes to sex are interesting with strong disapproval of adultery, and some relationships—particularly within the family or between a married man and a younger woman —are regarded as taboo. The attitude towards sex between unmarried men and women is very relaxed. Marriage for both sexes takes place at a much younger age than we are used to.

The tribes have an interesting attitude towards the up-bringing of children. Children are regarded as the responsibility of the community as a whole and adoptions often take place between families. Children are allowed to lead a very free life.

Their attitude towards inter-tribal conflict seems to be based on damage limitation. There is an emphasis on taking the enemy by surprise and breaking off hostilities after the first casualty. This means that population numbers are never seriously impacted. It also ensures a minimum of sustained contact between the tribes themselves. This has consequences for their language. Living on separate islands and having little or no communication with each other, the twelve Andamanese tribes each spoke their own language. These developed separately over the millennia and are still uninflected.

In looking at the Andaman islanders, one cannot help but meditate on them in their own right and on what we can learn from them that would be to our advantage. At a time of global warming, climate change, pollution, over-population and species loss, there seems to be quite a lot we could learn in terms of sustainable lifestyle, compatibility with the environment and what we might call 'social communism'. Most important, perhaps, is dancing—for them, a sure route to happiness.

I have spent most of my career promoting change in Africa and attempting to apply what I have always considered a universal truth: that we all gain from contact with other cultures, through learning from them and through the perspectives we stand to gain on our own values. The Africans I met have always been eager to learn and keen to modernize. They have also been more open to change than other cultures with which I have been in contact.

The Andamanese see things differently. Yet I find myself in as much sympathy with them as with Africans. It is not a question of incompatibility; the Andamanese simply hate and fear civilization and wish to keep their distance from it. Some 200 years since the arrival of the first settlers there has been not a single case of a native islander who sought to adopt or adapt to outside ways. The one case I know of where someone had the opportunity to leave his tribe was the Jarawa youth called Enmi whose badly broken leg had to be treated in the hospital in Port Blair. He adapted well to the life around him and had the option to stay in the city but decided without hesitation to go back to the forest.

Chapter 4

Islands out of This World

The Andamans, an archipelago of thickly wooded tropical islands in the Bay of Bengal, were unpopulated until 1857 apart from about 3,000 apparently stone-age aboriginals who wore no clothes and hunted with bows and arrows. The aboriginals had a reputation for killing any outsider venturing to their shores and since at least the days of the explorer Marco Polo, the world had left them alone. For centuries they killed sailors shipwrecked on their shores and would use metal from the ships to fashion their deadly arrow tips. To this day the Sentinelese, an Andamanese tribe who live on an island west of the main Andaman chain and speak a language spoken by nobody else, remain the only community in the world who still resist all contact with the outside world. Nobody even knows how many individuals there are; there may be as few as 50 or as many as 200.

The threat to the Andamans and to its people dates from 1857, following the Indian Mutiny of that year when shortage of space in mainland jails led the British to set up a penal settlement in the Andamans to accommodate the mutineers.

In November 2018 an American, John Chau, arrived in the islands on a tourist visa. He had made previous visits there, motivated by an obsession with bringing Jesus to the people of North Sentinel, the most remote island of the archipelago and inhabited by one of the smallest and fiercest of the twelve Andamanese tribes. As is customary with missionaries he had already travelled to some of the most remote places in the world, preaching to people about their sins and their need for redemption. Now he wanted to take on the ultimate challenge of bringing The Word of the Lord to the Sentinelese, the only community on the planet with no contact with other human beings.

Chau may not have known fully what he was taking on. In 1899 the then Andamans' commissioner, Sir Richard Temple (1850–1931), pursued a group of convicts who had from the settlement and made their way to North Sentinel. Temple landed on the island to find that all had been killed. He went on to describe the Sentinelese as 'a tribe which slays every stranger however inoffensive on sight, whether a forgotten member of itself, of another Andamanese tribe, or a complete foreigner.' This was, is, and always has been a very dangerous place.

Chau was a young man with a mission. He had been born in Alabama and was brought up on the north-west coast of the United States by a Chinese father and an American mother. From childhood he was consumed by two passions which became increasingly related: outdoor adventure and Jesus Christ. His hero was the explorer and missionary David Livingstone. Like his father, John graduated from Oral Roberts, an ultra-conservative evangelical university in Oklahoma which forbids smoking, drinking, swearing and sex outside marriage.

When he became aware of North Sentinel and a population that had never had the chance to know Christianity, Chau came to think of it as the ultimate challenge. In preparation he kept himself fit, travelled widely and had a series of adventures camping and climbing in the wildest places he could find. He also attended boot-camps such as one run by an organization in Kansas City that promised to see 'Jesus worshipped by every tongue, tribe and nation'.

In 2015 and 2016 Chau made four trips to the Andaman Islands and made contact with the local Christian community but did not attempt to visit North Sentinel. On a course at a missionary language school in Canada, he told a friend, Ben, of his 'burden' to save the Sentinelese. Ben wrote back to say he was convinced that only God could relieve Chau's burden. He said he already knew all the arguments why this was a fool's errand, but that they had not convinced him.

In October 2018, feeling that the time was ripe, Chau travelled to Port Blair, took up residence in a safe house and made contact with some Christian fisherman. They agreed to take him to North Sentinel, in contravention of a government ban on approaching closer than three miles. Chau assembled a response kit including picture cards for communications, dental forceps for removing arrows, and gifts such as tweezers, scissors, safety pins and fish hooks for the islanders. He documented his activities and his thoughts in a hand-written diary, knowing that he might be writing for posterity. Aware of the risk of infecting the Sentinelese with diseases that their bodies would not be able to resist, he subjected himself to 11 days of quarantine, during which he exercised, read and prayed.

On the night of 14 November Chau set off with the fishermen in a fishing boat carrying a kayak. It has been suggested that he had little idea of what he was doing or of the extreme dangers of his expedition. He was in fact well aware of them but felt called on by the Almighty to draw the attention of the Sentinelese to their godless plight and that the outcome, whatever it might be, would inevitably be an expression of God's will.

Chau wrote in his diary that the journey was illuminated by glowing plankton and that around them fish jumped like darting mermaids. The boat reached North Sentinel in the dark and anchored outside the reef.

At dawn the fishermen refused to take him nearer the shore so Chau stripped to his underwear, as he thought this might make the Sentinelese feel more at ease, and got into the kayak. He paddled it through a gap in the reef, headed for the long white line of coral sand in front of a solid green wall of enormous trees, and paddled towards a hut on the beach beside which were moored some canoes. As he approached several Sentinelese, faces painted yellow, came rushing out of the hut. He shouted from his kayak 'my name is John and I love you and Jesus loves you.' When the islanders began stringing their bows, he panicked and, according to his diary, 'turned and paddled like I never have in my life'.

Later that day he made another attempt, this time landing on the island and laying out gifts. He then approached the hut. About half a dozen Sentinelese emerged and began to whoop and shout. Chau tried to mimic their words back to them and they burst out laughing. He concluded that they were probably insulting him so he sang worshipful songs and preached from Genesis. For a while the islanders seemed to tolerate his presence. Then suddenly a boy fired an arrow which struck the cover of his bible and stuck. He pulled it out and handed it back to the boy and hastily retreated, only to find that his kayak had gone. In order to get away he had to swim for a kilometre all the way back to the fishing boat.

Back on board he started writing in his diary, describing the events of the day and confessing that he was scared. He was crying a bit and wondering if the beautiful sunset that he was watching was the last he would ever see 'before being in a place where the sun never sets'. Writing for his family to read he says, 'You guys might think I am crazy in all this but I think it's worth it to declare Jesus to these people.' He went on to ask God if this was 'Satan's last stronghold, where no one has heard or even had the chance to hear your name'.

Chau decided that he would make his next trip without the fishing boat nearby, as he felt this might make the islanders less nervous and would spare the fishermen the ordeal of having to bear witness to his death if things went badly. His diary makes it clear that he did not want to die, but accepted the possibility. He wrote, 'I think I would be more useful alive but to you God I give all the glory for whatever happens'. He asked God to 'forgive any of the people on this island who try to kill me. Shortly after dawn on 16 November, the last day he was seen alive, John Chau asked the fisherman to drop him off alone. As an article in the *Observer* put it, 'He knew the risks, but the people of North Sentinel were damned and he was determined to save them.'

Chapter 5
Joining the World

The background to John Chau's courageous but foolhardy foray goes back a long way. The Sentinelese have a reputation for killing outsiders, whether they be traders, settlers, missionaries or shipwrecked sailors. Of the handful of outsiders brave or foolish enough to risk rowing ashore, few have escaped with their lives. The reputation of North Sentinel, as well as the 40 miles of open sea separating the island from the main island chain, has been enough to keep people away.

Marco Polo, the Venetian merchant navigator born in 1254, was known as a braggart and an exaggerator and may not have reached China as he claimed. He is known, none the less, to have reached the Andaman Islands in the thirteenth century. He described the islanders as 'Oriental Negroes in the lowest state of barbarism who have remained in their isolated and degraded condition so near the shores of great civilized countries for so many ages. Rice and milk they have not and their fruits are the wild ones.' Polo went on to say the natives 'planted banyans and cocoa trees for their food.' Most of this is nonsense. The Andamanese were never cannibals, nor had they ever planted anything. Their colourful and false reputation was enhanced by an early Arab explorer quoted as saying 'the inhabitants of these islands eat men alive. They are black with woolly hair and in their eyes and countenance there is something quite frightful. They go naked and have no boats. If they had, they would devour all who passed near them.'

The notoriety that kept the world away was sustained and enhanced from the late eighteenth century by early British visitors, including the Royal Navy's Captain Archibald Blair, who joined the chorus by describing the islanders as the lowest form of human being and an unspeakable order of savages. He had been commissioned by the British Government in 1788 to carry out a survey with a view to the establishment of a settlement. This was set up on the south end of a fine natural harbour that he called Port Cornwallis. It was soon moved to an alternative location for health reasons and then abandoned altogether. The islands and their indigenous inhabitants continued their undisturbed life for the next half century.

In 1857 the penal colony referred to above was established on the abandoned site of Port Cornwallis, now renamed Port Blair. Its use began a relationship between Britain and the islands that was destined to remain more or less unchanged until Indian independence 90 years later.

At a time when Britain was rapidly accumulating other colonies, Britain's interest in the Andamans was relatively unusual. Elsewhere, colonies were developed because of the value that could be extracted from them, militarily or economically. In the Andamans, by contrast, the natives were thought to be of no value to the Empire and any major effort at establishing relations with them was therefore thought to be unproductive and wasteful. This seemed to suit both sides, though it also freed the British from trying to understand the indigenous population. Britain's view appeared to be that leaving the local people alone would make it easier to run the penal colony. What it failed to consider were the consequences of siting the new prison and Port Blair itself on an island inhabited by a particularly hostile tribe—the Jarawa.

Minor attempts to establish good relations with the Jarawa failed and it was not long before the Jarawa started to kill prisoners and their guards. Such was the priority given to the convicts that navigating the customs and language of the Jarawa was largely ignored. Records suggest there was virtually no contact at all with the tribespeople following their killing of convicts and settlers other than occasional and usually unsuccessful expeditions of reprisal.

One early and significant incident involving the Onge tribe on Little Andaman in the far south enhanced the notoriety of the Andaman tribes: it was their attack on a British military force sent by steamship to investigate the suspected murder of the crew of a small merchant vessel, Britain's *Assam Valley*, by Onge tribesmen on the island.

The event occurred in 1867 and involved another British ship, the *Arracan*, based in Rangoon, which sailed from Penang to Little Andaman with a hundred officers and men of the South Wales

Regiment. As the *Arracan* approached the shore it launched two boats, one of which foundered in the heavy surf just short of the beach. The soldiers managed to scramble ashore and soon discovered first a human skull, then several half-buried bodies, presumably *Assam Valley* crewmen.

Suddenly tribesmen appeared from the edge of the forest and fired arrows at the landing party. The soldiers responded with gunshot but things went badly wrong when they ran out of ammunition. They decided to withdraw but could not relaunch their boats and get back to their ship. Two rescue boats and several rafts were then launched but failed to get through the surf to the stranded soldiers, few of whom could swim.

At this point, the *Arracan's* assistant surgeon, Campbell Mellis Douglas, appeared on the scene. Douglas, a Canadian and expert boatman, steering a gig from its bows with four oarsmen, launched into the surf. The rescuers showed immense courage and presence of mind in a dangerous situation, with men including the chief officer of the *Arracan* in the water, surrounded by battered boats and rafts. Under a hail of arrows fired by angry tribesmen, Douglas dived in and, despite wounding himself on submerged rocks, saved the chief officer. Several other men were rescued and placed on rafts. In the end, only one officer was drowned.

All the others—17—were returned to the *Arracan*. For their bravery, Dr Douglas and his four oarsmen, all privates, received the newly-created Victoria Cross, the highest award for bravery in the empire. Few incidents before or since have received more such awards.

It now began to be understood that the Andamanese were people whose level of evolution and whose reaction to outsiders was of a different order from that of aboriginal people in British Africa, Borneo, Papua New Guinea and Australia. It also became apparent that these aboriginals, who looked like Africans, were not a single tribe. There were twelve tribes who not only spoke different languages but also had difficulty communicating with each other. This is one reason why they did not all come together to confront the British newcomers. They were also hampered by their inability to build sea-going boats.

Meanwhile, the importance of the Andamans as a penal colony was growing in line with the growth in inmate numbers and the desperation of those with little or no hope of eventual release.

Attempts to escape rose in number and were severely punished, often with death. Attempts to deter would-be escapees with a stricter regime also failed and it was only after the introduction of a positive regime that rewarded good behaviour and introduced education and skills training that behaviour and morale improved—and improved dramatically. This was the start of a system that gave convicts the self-esteem, training, experience and motivation to become pioneers in the building up of this new part of the Indian Empire.

It was at this time, at the end of the nineteenth century, that Col. Sir George Anson BT[1] (1848–1916) was military superintendent, under the commissionership of Temple. On the scene now arrived one Reginald Fendal Lowis, known as Reggie,[2] a thirty-one-year-old forester with the Indian Forestry Service on a routine posting from Burma to gauge the potential of the lush Andaman forests for commercial exploitation. Lowis met Anson, who obviously liked him, thought his talents were wasted on forestry and used his influence to arrange a transfer for him to the Andamans Commission. This meant entry into the Indian Civil Service (ICS), which he was destined to serve for the rest of his working life.

Anson also introduced Lowis to his niece Bessie Coldstream,[3] then in her late teens, who kept house for him, organizing the local servants to carry out the housework—cleaning and cooking—while leaving to herself more refined jobs such as flower arranging. The introduction of Lowis to Bessie took place in 1898 and it brought the three families even closer together. The Ansons, Coldstreams and Lowises, from Edinburgh and the Borders, already had records of service in India going back generations to the East India Company; they became even more intertwined when Bessie and Lowis got married. The match seemed propitious: both loved wild places and nowhere was wilder than the Andamans. As a couple they could look forward to travel in the islands as well the rich social life for which Port Blair was well known. Four children followed, all born in the Andamans, of whom the first was Elizabeth.[4]

Lowis seems to have been an instant success. By Indian Civil Service (ICS) standards he was relatively mature with ten years'

---

[1] The author's great-great-uncle.

[2] The author's grandfather.

[3] The author's grandmother.

[4] The author's mother.

Col. Sir George Anson BT, seated. The Andaman Islands military superintendent.

experience of India and appeared to everyone to be well suited to working with people. He lacked only the ICS administrator's traditional Oxbridge background but made up for this with his level-headedness and good judgement. From the start, in contrast to the three or four years spent by most administrators on the islands, he was earmarked to provide continuity and went on to spend more than two decades in the Andamans. For much of the time he acted as commissioner and lived in Government House on Ross Island at the entrance to the harbour (*see old engravings, next page*).

In addition to serving as one of the islands' administrators and magistrates, Lowis helped set up trading links between the British

Top: View of Ross Island. Above: Government House at the top of Ross Island.

and the Great Andamanese tribes of Middle and North Andaman in such local products as tortoise shell, mother of pearl and trepan. These trades were almost the only pretext for contact between the British and the tribes. Lowis made up for this by initiating cautious family visits to coastal villages, which were in due course reciprocated, but there was otherwise a general indifference to the need to understand tribal customs and culture, and only minimal effort to establish cooperation and maintain working relationships.

The situation for the aboriginal people received new, more professional attention with the arrival of Alfred Radcliffe-Brown, a

'Shameful': Radcliffe-Brown's work aroused a new curiosity about the islanders.

brilliant and ground-breaking young Cambridge anthropologist, to do research. Radcliffe-Brown carried out a two-year study of the tribal customs and way of life of the Great Andamanese between 1906 and 1908 and wrote a book which remains the most authoritative and professional study ever carried out on them.

In the wake of Radcliffe-Brown, curiosity about the tribespeople increased. Individuals started being kidnapped and carried off to Calcutta or Penang in an attempt to educate them, study them and convert them to western ways. Such experiments were not only shameful in their disregard of the autonomy and human rights of the islanders but also a total failure. When the captives were returned to the Andamans all died of the diseases they had contracted, to which they had no immunity.

Lowis, now an assistant commissioner, was given charge of the 1911 census of the islands. He was able to travel their length and breadth, making head counts in the case of the friendly and relying on estimates in the case of the hostile. Comparing figures with those of the census ten years earlier, he was the first administrator to appreciate the devastating impact of newcomers, British and Indian, on the aboriginal population. He was shocked. In his very full report, he blamed 'civilization' in general and the arrival of diseases such as measles, influenza and syphilis in particular.

Above: Andaman Islands women by their huts. Detail below: all smoke pipes.

During the 1911 census Lowis built up an unrivalled knowledge of the Andaman and Nicobar islands. His census team visited North Sentinel for the first time since Temple's ten years earlier but found it too dangerous to attempt a count. No attempt was made to carry out a count of the Sentinelese during the next census in 1921.

The British also started to become aware that the native hunter-gatherer population had a special but unfathomable relationship with nature. Although sophisticated in their taste for local fruits, roots, honey and fish, they were incapable of learning modern agricultural techniques or responding to any sort of training or basic education. They simply could not change. Lowis wondered why this was, and looked for answers in their origins. They were clearly very different in appearance from the inhabitants of the great Asian land masses around them, and their lifestyle was different too. Lowis thought they looked like Africans. But if they were so, how could they have reached the Andamans, and when?

Lowis worried, meanwhile, about the drastic decline in their population and blamed the British for failing to try to understand them better. This led him to make further private attempts to contact the friendlier tribes in North Andaman and Rutland Islands, some resulting in events that his wife Bessie and her children would remember for the rest of their lives.

He was particularly concerned about the attitude of the Jarawa tribe. They lived in areas right up to the edges of the settlement and, besides killing convicts and their guards, had taken to raiding crops that were being cultivated to feed the community. He felt that their continuing hostility towards authority would lead to their early demise, but did not yet recognize that the hostility of the Jarawa and the Sentinelese was self-protective. At a time when syphilis and measles were decimating the Great Andamanese, the Jarawa remained unaffected.

The 1911 census was a turning point in Lowis's career. He was already an assistant commissioner. Now he gained promotion to deputy commissioner and spent increasing periods acting as commissioner. He started to play a leading role in shaping all aspects of government policy, including putting convicts to work in the coffee and rubber plantations, thereby bringing their labour into the islands' economy.

In 1916 Reggie and Bessie returned home on leave, which meant a dangerous sea voyage of three weeks' duration. By now their oldest children, Elizabeth and Janet, were at boarding school in England and leave meant they could reunite with their Lewis and Coldstream relations. Once back in England, Reggie wanted to join up but was told that it was more important that he return to the Andamans. Due to his fluency in German, however, he was given a temporary job censoring mail between Britain and Germany. His return to the Andamans was followed by increasingly wide responsibilities and longer periods acting as commissioner. It was not until the end of the war that another opportunity arose to visit home again.

Another India-wide census took place in 1921 with Lowis again taking direct charge of the Andamans and Nicobars. Again his comprehensive report was published in book form and revealed a continuing fall in the population of all the tribes except the Jarawa.

Following his retirement the next year, Lowis and Bessie moved to Canada. He had given the Andamans 21 years' service and his legacy was considerable. Beyond the dry statistics of his census data from 1911 and 1921, his books reveal a deep interest in all the aspects of this remote island chain and its administrative needs. The books also show that he was honest enough to acknowledge both government failings and his own. Reading between the lines, he seems to have blamed himself for not encouraging other officials to develop the communication skills necessary to maintain a degree of mutual understanding with the tribespeople. Radcliffe-Brown would eventually draw attention to the ravages of imported diseases, but his book did not appear until 1922, and it was Lowis whose reports should first have raised alarm bells. He was clearly shocked by the scale of fatalities and seems to have blamed himself for not noticing the scale of the problem at the time. He summarizes his own and the British role when he writes 'It was not recognized until too late that to bring a people like the Andamanese too suddenly under the influence of civilization was altogether harmful.'

Bessie's legacy included a number of articles on the realities of living and working in the Andamans and Nicobars: descriptions of social and club life, the wonders of marine life among the coral, the hunt for a deadly killer shark, speculation on the future abolition of the death penalty. Several of these writings were published in Indian newspapers or in British periodicals. Some appear as appendices to this book.

Bessie's younger daughter Mary returned from India to Ross Island, her place of birth, in 1930 after marrying a newly appointed assistant commissioner of police, Roo Deane. They stayed for four years. By now Indian Nationalist activity was gaining ground and the convict population reflected that. The new Indian settler population was growing rapidly, and the islands were becoming more prosperous.

During the Second World War, India contributed the biggest volunteer army in the history of the world to help the British. The Andamans were not directly affected until an unrelated tragedy occurred: an earthquake that destroyed almost all the buildings on Ross Island. The Japanese then took the opportunity to invade the islands, imposing a brutal regime of torture and execution on the hundreds of settlers whom they had expected would sympathize and cooperate with them as liberators from British rule. The Japanese even brought Netaji ('respected leader') Subhas Chandra Bose to the islands in the hope of his winning over the Andamanese settlers. Bose, an extreme Indian patriot, led the Indian National Army (INA) and had initial success in recruiting Indian turncoats but failed to survive the reversal in British military fortunes from late 1944, and the settler population remained overwhelmingly hostile to the Japanese-backed insurgency.

The Japanese paid little attention to the tribes but carried out bombing raids, particularly on the Jarawa whom they wrongly suspected of harbouring British infiltrators. The Japanese suspicion that the British were able to maintain a presence on the main islands throughout the war was true but it was provided by special service soldiers from the British Indian Army, whom the Japanese never identified. These forces had no contact with the natives and though they encountered parties of Jarawa tribesmen on more than one occasion, there was no engagement between them

Independence for India and the Andamans came in 1947. Indian government policy towards the tribes continued basically unchanged with commitments to safeguard the culture and way of life of the aboriginals. Change came however with the arrival of new Indian settlers—at first mainly ex-servicemen who were allowed to build and cultivate particularly in parts of South Andaman on land the Jarawa tribe regarded as theirs. There then ensued years of crop raiding and clashes, resulting in the unravelling of Indian commitment to preserving the tribes' culture and way of life, and all the damage that has followed since the bulding of the trunk road.

Chapter 6
Research

My wish to visit the Andamans with my daughter Juliet was partly inspired by my family's connection with them, by the stories of my mother Elizabeth, by the key role played by my grandfather Reginald Lowis, and by his books and the articles written by my grandmother Bessie, combined with my curiosity about the British Empire which had shaped my early life. I had always wanted to know more about these islands, their unmatched aboriginal inhabitants and their energetic and creative settlers and finally I decided I must go and explore them for myself. We set off in May 2018.

One thing that motivated me further was the reticence of various agencies when I approached them for information. In spite of my explaining my family involvement with India and the islands, and my deep concern for the future of the aboriginal tribes, agency staff seemed far less helpful than I had expected. It was then that I started to become aware of conflicting and intertwined sensitivities. Some of these evidently had to do with the survival of the Andamanese environment and its people but others had more to do with money and big business, national pride, sovereignty, and the authority of the courts. As I write this, I appreciate that the Indian government wishes not to compromise its autonomy to the interference of well-meaning do-gooders, but I am convinced that India would do best for itself and the Andamans by facing up to the issues. India needs to attract the world's understanding and help in deciding how to go forward rather than remaining in its current logjam of strategic indecision and giving the impression of being tragically misguided and uncaring.

Exploring my family history with Juliet would be fairly straight-forward, I thought. The things I wanted to see were all mapped out for me by what my mother had told me and what I read about my grandparents' preoccupations and predictions. I knew that, a century on, the way things looked on the ground—modern Port Blair, modern Ross Island, the Cellular Jail, the island jungles and empty beaches—would be very different from what I had imagined, but I was sure that local people, especially the descendants of settlers and former convicts and others with an interest in the future of the islands and its indigenous inhabitants, would be able to join up the dots for me. I was confident, too, that they would be able to amplify material I had found on the internet and in the Indian section of the British Library about my family's record, and more widely that of the British, and reveal to me how we—a historical phenomenon—were now viewed: an odd thought.

What would be more more difficult was discovering more about the Andamans' extraordinary hunter-gatherers: their past, their present and their prospects. What was known about them, who had done what work on them, and how had that work not affected them? Were there tribespeople in other parts of the world with whom they could be compared, knowledge of whom made it possible to make safe anthropological generalizations, or was one forced to fall back largely on informed guesswork? One thing I was under no illusions about. From all I had read over the previous six months, there was no chance of my laying eyes on a native Andamanese. If doing so was so compromising to them, I would not want to, in any case. That was a red line.

I had always been aware of the impact that life on the islands had had on my mother and her brother and sisters. She had woken my imagination from earliest childhood with stories of the beauty and romance of an unknown part of the world inhabited by these small, naked, loving little people. She told me too about how she and her brother and sisters had been spoiled by some of the Sikh convicts, the inmates of the vast penal colony who had trained as guards, gardeners and maintenance workers at Government House.

Before she died in 1977, my mother had given me a file of papers labelled 'RFL's Articles'. Now reading them for the first time, I found they were mainly short stories and descriptions of life in Canada after grandfather's retirement but included among them were Granny Bessie's handwritten articles dating from 1896 to 1922. These included descriptions of life in mainland India, camping trips deep inside remote jungles and a tiger hunt organized by her father on the Nepalese border in 1886. Of her raft of articles about life in the

Bessie Coldstream's account of an Indian tiger hunt, published 21 November 1903.

Andaman Islands, some were original and handwritten and others were cuttings from Indian newspapers and British journals such as *The Ladies' Field*. I devoured them all with the greatest interest. They told of club life in Port Blair, explorations of the sea shore with her children and an encounter with a huge shark. There were also insights into British policy towards the 13,000 convicts and the role they played in the life of the islands. Disappointingly, there was little mention of the aboriginal islanders.

More detail on our family's history in the islands came from my cousin Tim Deane, the son of Elizabeth's younger sister Mary. Mary, like my mother, was born on Ross Island and had by extraordinary coincidence returned there as a newly-wed in 1930 with her husband Roo Deane when he was appointed an assistant commissioner of police. So it was that Tim, too, was born on Ross Island and went on to the Kashmir boarding school which I was sent to four years later, during the Second World War. Tim then decided on a military career and flew helicopters in the Army Air Corps. Like me his childhood in India became a major influence in his life. He sent me some hundred-year-old photographs of his mother and our uncle John playing with aboriginal children, as well as the transcript of a BBC talk she gave before she died, about expeditions to outer islands and races with tribal children on the backs of turtles (*see Appendix 6*). Tim also provided some interesting details of his father's achievements on the islands and the way he was regarded by the settler community.

Another first cousin, Iain Lowis, son of Uncle John who during the Second World was a colonel in the Ghurkhas with the author

John and Mary Lowis holding hands with aboriginal tribeschildren. Photo 1913.

John Masters, sent me more photographs. Iain, who had himself become a colonel and commanded The King's Own Scottish Borderers, gave me a photo of Onge tribespeople arriving by canoe to present Granny and Grandfather with some dugong tusks.

All this was whetting my appetite and now it was time to find out what details I could glean on my family's role in the Andamans from the Indian Office section of the British Library, beside St Pancras Station in London. Aunt Mary had always told me that she knew it well and that it was a mine of information. First I had to obtain membership and, this gained, I spent two days in London consulting staff lists and annual reports on the Andaman and Nicobar Islands. First there were ICS career details on grandfather Reginald and his father and grandfather. There was similar information about my grandmother's Coldstream father and grandfather. I also learned a lot about my grandmother's uncle Sir George Anson, former military superintendent in the Andamans for whom Granny Bessie was keeping house when she met Reginald. Aunt Mary's husband Roo Deane of the Indian Police featured too, as did my father Wilfred of the Indian Service of Engineers. None of this information gave any personal details—opinions, personalities, private lives—but I was lucky to have Bessie's articles and my mother's long memoir of her father, which filled in a lot of gaps. Beyond that I had my own childhood memories of family members and of India.

The British Library also held copies of government reports on the Andamans that I was able to link to family members. There were statistics on how prisoners in the days of my grandfather's administration were employed in every part of the economy from government service of every sort to farming and the production of food for a growing population. I noted the emphasis on enterprise and the encouragement given to convicts to start businesses. Here was a vibrant, active, largely self-sufficient, community. Interesting too was information on new plantations pioneering crops such as rubber, tea, coffee and rice; data on illness and deaths in the prison hospital; and details of the crimes committed by male and female prisoners during my grandfather's era. Here I observed that whatever the political nature of inmates' crimes before and since, the prison was not used to punish political agitation *per se* in Grandfather's time.

Until now I did not know what my grandfather had thought of

Bessie's uncle George Anson: encouraged RFL to join the Andamans Commission.

all this. I knew however that he played a pivotal role in the administration at an important time and had got on well with the aboriginal tribes. Beyond that I went on to learn from the internet something I had missed in the India Office Library: his supervision of the two censuses of 1911 and 1921 and the books he had written in their wake. I ordered both books at once and gained valuable insights into the history of the islands and aspects of island life for which there is no other record. Most interesting were what he had written at the time and on the spot about his own and his generation's attitudes and perspectives. To me they indicated a practical, reasoned and humane approach towards the convicts as well as the indigenous inhabitants, who proved a continuing challenge for a long-suffering administration.

Grandfather Reginald quotes the censuses to show the impact on the islands of the free Indian settlers and released convicts, whose numbers were growing steadily in response to their growing role in the islands' economic activity. But even more significant is his recognition of what the censuses revealed about the aboriginal population. There was little that was not known at the time about the administrators, the convicts, the military and the free settlers, and so the reports give only the barest details about them, but Lowis's writings reveal a deep interest in the future of the islanders, in their attitude to the government and in their state of health in response to diseases brought in by newcomers. Revealing too is what he has to say about possible 'mainstreaming' or acculturation after witnessing the reaction of tribespeople to steps taken by the government to try to educate and train them for the modern world. He is devastating in what he has to say about efforts to 'civilize'.

Grandfather's books start with details of the geography and history of the Andaman and Nicobar Islands. They go on to describe aspects of tribal life and of relations with what had become known as the friendly tribes, as well as the authority's punitive raids, particularly on the unfriendly Jarawa, in retaliation for their killing of convicts and guards, and to deter crop-stealing raids.

During the censuses, as recorded earlier, Lowis and those other officers seconded to him for the census had travelled by boat to all parts of the islands, camping, shooting teal and pigeons, catching tuna and barracuda, and spearing turtles, all for the pot, when they weren't working. Though they could only estimate the numbers of the more hostile tribes, Lowis's writings show how profoundly shocked he was by his own evidence of the catastrophic decline in the numbers of the indigenous population. He made abundantly clear in one of his books what he considered the cause was: 'Civilization'!

I managed to get a copy of the anthropologist Alfred Radcliffe-Brown's book *The Andaman Islanders: a Study in Social Anthropology*, based on his two-year study of the Great Andamanese between 1906 and 1908. It was the first significant project of his career and one of which he says, 'It is indeed an apprentice work for it was through my work in the Andamans that I really learned anthropology.' The book is the only comprehensive professional study of the islanders undertaken before or since. The remarkable detail on all aspects of tribal life, customs and beliefs came just as the nine northern tribes were plunging towards extinction. I found the book remarkable for its detail. Radcliffe-Brown must have been a communicator of the first order. Whether he could have gleaned much from trying to work with the other three tribes at that time is doubtful. He says that in some ways he would have preferred to have been working on Little Andaman with the Onge but had to give up as the language problem was insurmountable. Thanks to the trade in local products with India, however, some of the Great Andamanese had a smattering of Hindi and this made communication possible.

I turned again to the internet to read what the University of Leicester historian Dr Clare Anderson had to say about the islands. She had been in touch with my sister Veronica and me several years earlier and I had given her copies of my grandmother's articles. Now she was helpful in drawing my attention to what she has since written about the history of contacts between the indigenous Andamanese and the outside world. She has also written about the Andamans in the context of their having been developed economically partly by ex-convicts, like Australia and Mauritius.

My sister Veronica had paid a visit to the islands in 2012 and had been guided by Dr Francis Neelam, the head of the local college, with his special interest in the history of the islands. I emailed him about my own planned visit and he promised to give me all possible help and cooperation. He also warned of acute government sensitivity to outside interest in its policy towards the tribes. As a former district commissioner in Africa—the last white British D.C. in Zambia after independence—and a specialist in the developing indigenous managers in Africa, I was greatly concerned by this. It suggested a government that had something to hide and that wished to head off foreign pressure. I was keen to get a better feel for this because the implications were so worrying. I was beginning to suspect that international opposition—the very thing the Indians least wanted —might be the only thing likely to save the Jarawa.

Thanks to my own experience as a happy Raj child in pre independence India (now Pakistan), in pre- and post-independence Mauritius and in colonial and post-colonial Africa, I had strong views about all three and about Britain's capacity for beneficial intervention which I tended to see in the most positive light. My mother Elizabeth had always told me that we sent our very best people into the Indian Civil Service and as a child I had heard and seen nothing to contradict that view. What I saw of the Colonial

Service in Africa was also of civil servants who loved the countries and the people they served and, virtually to a man or a woman, took great pride in the service's achievements.

My views on the subject had found focus in a programme of seminars run by London University and the Overseas Pensioners Society (OSPA), which attempted to bring together British academics and elderly former colonial civil servants. Many of the latter turned up, keen to talk to anyone who would listen about their career experiences; but the very academics who ought to have welcomed their first-hand testimonies seemed not to want to listen and mostly stayed away. Though eager to document the oral history of people in almost every other field of life, they seemed to think they had nothing to learn about the lives of specialists in this particular sector.

I was planning to draw attention to what I saw as invalid generalizations and comparisons. It seemed to me to be high time for those who could still provide essential eye-witness accounts of an earlier age to counter the prevailing ideological rigidity that Britain should be ashamed of her imperial role. It came as a shock, therefore, to start to discover that in the case of the Andaman Islands, the happy situation that I had known had a slightly more chequered history.

My excursions into the internet made me aware of the interest taken in the Andamans by Erika Hagelberg, a British evolutionary geneticist and professor of Biosciences, formerly based in Norway, who, while working at Cambridge, had discovered the Andamanese hair collected by Alfred Radcliffe-Brown and had examined its DNA. There were also details of the Indian DNA diagnostician Dr Lalji Singh, who accompanied Professor Hagelberg on a trip to the Andamans with the intention of carrying out more research on tribal genetic profiling.

Of great interest was the work of an Indian anthropologist, Triloknath (T.N.) Pandit, born in 1934 and a disciple of Radcliffe Brown, who in the 1960s was the first person to have any contact with the Jarawa. Pandit went on to establish a unique relationship with the Sentinelese, learning to communicate with them as both parties bobbed up and down in the sea just offshore. Also vital was a diary that I found in Port Blair during my visit in mid-2018 by an Indian government physician, Dr Ratan Chandra Kar, who in recent times has worked with the Jarawa, speaks their language and has gained their confidence. The diary, published in Bengali in 2009 and then in English as *The Jarawas of the Andamans* in 2013, contains much detail about the Jarawa culture and way of life and gives its author's views of the impact of the illegal Andaman Trunk Road, built down the spine of the islands.

After these researches, including a long article about the British military expedition that rescued the crew of the *Assam Valley*, referred to earlier, and a book about the Japanese invasion and of the islands between 1942 and 1945, I felt more motivated and somewhat better qualified to write something that might draw more attention to the plight of the Jarawa and the background to their predicament, and that might make a contribution to preventing the looming tragedy of their extinction. But first I needed to explore the islands.

Chapter 7

A Visit in 2018

All my life I have associated the Andamans with my mother's accounts of visits to remote islands and being embraced by stone-age tribespeople. More recently my imagination has been caught by my grand-mother's hundred-year-old articles about what life there was like for the British living in this remote and little-known but very special part of the Raj when it was still a penal settlement.

Most recently I have been thinking about how the aboriginal tribes have become aware of their predicament and all the changes that have arisen from the construction of the ATR and the arrival of the tourists. Apart from Granny's and Aunt Mary's articles I have read what academics such as professors Erika Hagelberg and Clare Anderson have written about their experiences and the history of the Andamans. I was also held spellbound by what Grandfather Reggie had written in his two accounts of the census of 1911 and 1921 which, to my surprise, I found were still available online.

The more I read the more I was fascinated by the story of the tribes, about whom the outside world knows little more now than did my grandparents and their friends and colleagues a century ago. Professor Hagelberg's recent discoveries have certainly alerted the world in a way no one else had done recently but mostly the Indian Government continues to stand aside while the depredations of the Jarawa continue. In one small way, the ignorance of the outside world has given the Jarawa a small degree of protection by helping to keep them isolated, but their security—already threatened by the three main dangers that Reggie Lowis identified: measles, syphilis and civilization—now includes settlement and tourism, as we have seen.

Though I had never been to the Andamans before 2018, I felt that my own background of birth and childhood in India, and my career background in Her Majesty's Overseas Civil Service, gave me a head start in the quest to understand some of the issues and complexities on the ground. In particular I found myself questioning some current writings and the tendency to draw parallels between the Andamans and other examples of British colonialism. In my view, the case of the Andamans is quite distinct and not a colonial stereotype.

I have hinted already at my criticism of career academics, their lack of experience of lived realities, their over-hasty imposition of theory and their often anachronistic application of today's values to past eras. Fearing accusations, however, that I was pontificating on a subject in which I had no direct experience, having not been in a position to go and live on the islands myself, and encouraged by my friend, the *Financial Times*'s former Africa editor Michael Holman, I felt I must gain some necessary perspective by paying a visit, and the sooner the better. I had a lot to learn and many questions to ask.

I had planned to travel with my wife Sarah but she was unwell, so my daughter Juliet stepped in to fill the breach. We flew to Port Blair pretty painlessly via Chennai (formerly Madras), where we boarded a plane full of Indian tourists. Francis Neelam, the contact whom my sister Veronica had introduced me to, was going to be away but he had put me in touch with a fellow academic, Dr Rashida Iqbal, curator of the former Cellular Jail and its library. She however had been called to Kolkata, so we were at a loss for informed contacts.

I had read on the internet about the editor of a local Andaman newspaper, the *Andaman Chronicle*. Denis Giles had strong views on the daily tourist trade along the Andaman Trunk Road and considered it unworthy and exploitative. He had written sympathetically about the tribes and been critical of the daily convoys of buses, which treated them like animals in a safari park. Since our time in Port Blair was going to be limited I decided to telephone him from Chennai airport about a meeting the next morning. I explained our mission and he agreed immediately.

We had left Heathrow on a Sunday afternoon in May. It was now a cloudless morning the next day and we were two hours out of Chennai over the Bay of Bengal. We would soon be landing in the country of my birth for the first time in 72 years. The sky was clear but there was nothing to see. Then suddenly way below us appeared a green island quite alone in the turquoise vastness of the Indian ocean. It was roughly square, about seven miles by six, and surrounded by white coral sand and light blue shallows protected by a dark coloured reef from dark blue of the ocean. It was more or less flat and appeared pristine and untouched by human hand.

With a great rush of excitement I recognized the shape. It was North Sentinel Island, yet to become notorious internationally for the murder of John Chau. I knew it housed one of the only communities on the planet that avoided all contact with the rest of the world—fierce forest-dwelling black people who looked like pygmies. Looking down from the skies, I tried to see evidence of their existence but there was none.

Soon came views of many more islands of varying sizes all heavily wooded and hilly, unlike North Sentinel, some with dwellings dotted among the dark green of the deep forest. Before long we were coming down to land at Port Blair.

Once out of the airport we took a taxi and headed for the Fortune Bay Resort Hotel which Francis Neelham had recommended. I tried to picture the Port Blair of my mother's day, spread out and verdant with greenery stretching to the bay where sharks lurked. I was keen to see the site of the golf course— one of the oldest in the world outside Britain—where my grandparents played in the first decade of the twentieth century. I asked our driver. He told us the course still existed but was in an area now controlled by the Indian Navy and was closed to the public.

The roads of Port Blair were dominated by tuk-tuks, half motorcycle, half motorcar, with room for two passengers and a little luggage. We swerved and braked to avoid suicidal motorbikes and pedestrians, as well as cows, sometimes lying in the road or chewing the cud on traffic islands.

Then we were driving up hill and down to our hotel. It was a delight: open-sided, set on high ground among trees, with wonderful views over the bay to untouched forest and what I recognized as Mount Harriet. To the right and in the middle of the bay was Ross Island, guarding the entrance to the harbour, and beyond Ross more islands including the long outline of Havelock in the far distance, 20 or 30 miles beyond.

The manager of the Fortune Bay Resort gave us a special welcome and we were delighted with our rooms, which looked out over gardens and coconut palms along the shore line. By now it was evening and we repaired to the open-sided bar for a drink and to discuss our programme. A charming young Nicobarese was singing songs from my youth. Noticing my enthusiasm as we crossed the floor to our table, she invited me to join her in singing 'The Tennessee Waltz', which brought smiles to fellow guests, mostly middle-class Indian business people or tourists from the mainland, some with children. We went down the steps to dine in the open air dining room and before bed arranged for a taxi to take us to the *Andaman Chronicle* offices early next day.

The next morning after breakfast a huge bearded man called Aziz introduced himself. He was to be our driver. While driving he told us that he was a Muslim and that a great-grandfather had been imprisoned by the British in the Cellular Jail. This was just the sort of contact I was hoping to make, and I was fascinated to hear of pride in India's multiculturalism. Aziz went on to drive us to all our appointments over the rest of the week. The first was to Denis Giles, the *Andaman Chronicle*'s youthful editor. He could not have been more welcoming. With him in his office were two students from Hyderabad University studying journalism.

From the outset I could see that Denis was open minded and not afraid to express opinions that might conflict with local or national politics. Clearly he had a special interest in the tribes and was most unhappy with the effect of tourism and the Andaman Trunk Road on the Jarawa. We talked too about the impact on the Jarawa of settlers now living next to their reserves and sometimes clashing with them. He confirmed my impression that the Andamans were at a crossroads with authority, both Indian and Andaman, and that there were uncertainties about the way ahead. Clearly the issues and pressures were huge.

I asked who else shared Denis's views and whether we could meet them. What was government policy: was there any official line? What recent contacts had there been with the Jarawa and the Sentinelese? Did they really not play any part at all in the life of the modern Andamans? What had been learned about them and what could we learn from them? And what about public opinion? I also wondered about the past: how Britain's historic role in the islands was viewed, and how the British had shaped their growth and development. I expressed concern that there should be effective international pressure on India and that my interest might be of value.

Denis put us in touch with other settlers whose families had been on the islands for generations and who, like Uncle Roo Deane, husband of Aunt Mary, were members of the 'Local Born Society'.

These were the people who I sensed would provide the most balanced perspective. Denis also revealed that, like Aziz, he was descended from convict stock—and proud of it. I started to think a lot more about the influences of my grandfather, about British policy towards the convicts and about the role they played in the islands.

Before parting, Denis arranged for the female student, Ambika, to interview me the next day for the *Chronicle* and we invited him and the two students to dine with us at the hotel before we left to spend our last two nights on Havelock Island.

Near the top of our visit programme was Ross Island where Granny and Grandfather had lived for long periods, much of that time in Government House when he was acting commissioner, and where Mum and her sisters and brother had all been born. It was much nearer the mainland than I had imagined—less than half a mile by ferry. As we approached the jetty, apart from some sheds on the shore, there was no sign of any buildings under the canopy of the enormous trees.

Having landed, Juliet and I decided to walk everywhere so we were not troubled by the crowds of tourists. We immediately struck a path up to the top of the hill. Though the trees dominated the landscape nothing grew beneath them—no saplings or shrubs, no flowers, not even grass. This made for a bleak bare landscape. Then we saw the cause: large deer of an introduced Chinese variety, we were told, that ate anything they could reach. I would rather have had the vegetation than the deer.

Adding to the general bleakness of the scene was a different type of decimation. Ross Island had suffered a massive earthquake in 1941, many years after our family had lived there, and most of its buildings had been reduced to near rubble. We made first for the Anglican Church (wrongly called Presbyterian on the plaque). It was a sad sight that greeted us. It had been a big church and although there was no longer a roof, the walls, still standing, seemed to be prevented from crumbling by massive intertwining creepers. There was no sense of any sort of sanctity.

We moved on to Government House. Clearly it had been a grand house. The terrazzo flooring of the hall and living-room had survived but nothing else except a few walls with creepers. There was no sign of a lawn or a garden. I found it impossible to imagine the

The Anglican Church on Ross Island: held up 'by massive intertwining creepers'.

grand manicured landscape through which the Lewis children played and rode their ponies under the watchful eye of turbaned retainers.

I looked for the prison cell from which came the cries of the prisoner condemned to death that had so moved Granny (*see Appendix 3*) but could find no trace. Perhaps she had meant Viper Island. The only building we saw that was more or less intact was the barracks which had housed the garrison of British soldiers and, later, the Japanese invaders in the Second World War.

Overall I was more saddened than stimulated. Had Ross Island survived I would have enjoyed a dreamlike stroll into the past, with the sights bringing back to life my mother's and my grandmother's writings.

As Juliet and I walked back along the path to the ferry, we got talking to a couple from New Delhi. They too were disappointed, though they showed a lot more interest when I told them about our family connection. They had travelled up the ATR the previous day to see the tribespeople. They were not disappointed. Their bus had stopped beside a child standing beside the road. The driver had handed over a packet of biscuits, while telling the passengers that it was only he who was allowed to give out gifts.

Back in Port Blair we went to another favoured tourist destination, the Cellular Jail, now a national monument commemorating

The Cellular Jail (1896–1906): only three of the original seven wings now stand.

India's independence struggle. It was the newly-built prison where in my grandparents' day the prisoners spent their first months in custody. Now, besides having been turned into a museum, there was also a library where we introduced ourselves to the librarian whom Rashida Iqbal had advised us to see. She showed us original copies of my grandfather's two *Census of India* tomes of 1911 and 1921, both in the original form in which they had published. She confirmed that they are among the most important books ever written about the administration of the islands, their history and geography, and their indigenous inhabitants.

The Cellular Jail, built from 1896 to 1906, had originally been massive, at one time accommodating some 13,000 prisoners. It had the classical form of a panopticon, with corridors of cells like spokes of a wheel coming together at a central tower, which made it possible for the guards to monitor the whole complex. Though now reduced to two spokes with three floors of individual cells, it was still impressive and had been well maintained. A building built between the spokes housed pictures of the jail from earlier days and contained other memorabilia reflecting what had obviously been a harsh regime. Much was made of a particular superintendent whose large chair, almost a throne, was on show. From there he would apparently rail at the prisoners, to frighten them and impress them with his power. We climbed to the top of the central tower where there were numerous displays listing political prisoners. I found this puzzling because what I had seen in annual reports in the India Office Library suggested that the crimes committed by prisoners in my grandfather's time were mostly murder, rape and 'dacoitry'— violent robbery committed by an armed gang—none of which could be classed as political.

Our first visit the next day was to the Anthropological Department and its museum next door. At first it seemed that the head of the department was unavailable but while we were looking round the museum, a messenger called us back and we were led into the director's office. It seemed that he had started work in the Andamans only a few weeks earlier and a little lacking in experience. He seemed excited when I told him about my grandparents and the reason for our visit but unimpressed by my objection to government policy on the tribes, and to the wish not to involve foreign advisers. He told us he shared my worries about contact between the settlers and the Jarawa on South and Middle Andaman but was unable to express an opinion on the effect of the ATR, and thought that banning visits by foreign anthropologists to see the tribes was nonsense. Above all he seemed to want to assert himself in his new position. He was due to return to the mainland the next day for a conference in Kolkata and urged me to accompany him, even offering to pay my fare, an offer I had to decline. I was disappointed by his unfamiliarity with official policy towards the tribespeople and by the prognosis for their future.

We then went to the Tribal Research Office which looks into all matters affecting the tribes, including the impact of tourism. Here we met four members of staff, all female. Perhaps because their male boss was away, or because Juliet was with me, the women seemed to speak more freely than they might otherwise have done. All agreed that the Jarawa were increasingly affected by contact with settlers now living in areas adjacent to them, and by tourism along the ATR. Clearly they felt there was a great deal at stake here, not least the possibility of early extinction. That said, one of the women had the honesty to admit that although contact with the outside world was the last thing the Jarawa needed, she would love to have met a tribesperson, something her colleagues all agreed with.

Our next two visits were particularly memorable. My late uncle Roo had belonged to the revered Local Born Society—indeed, his role in putting out a fire at the Aberdeen Bazaar, Port Blair's commercial centre, brought him election to honorary membership of the society, which gave me the perfect introduction when meeting current members. The first was Mukeshwar Lall, a local film maker, historian and collector, and the owner of the superbly conceived and maintained Kalapani Museum on the outskirts of Port Blair, on the road north towards the ATR. Lall was a delight— charming, patriotic, helpful and very well informed. You felt that the future of the archipelago and its tribes would be in safer hands, were he in charge, than it is at present. His museum is extensive, taking up three floors, with hundreds of photos and other memorabilia. It includes several life-size montages of forest workers of my grandfather's era being attacked and killed by tribesmen. Included among the photos was one of the Local Born Society in 1934 and there was Roo Deane in the picture.

We stayed at Kala Pani (*kaala paanee*; 'black water'—words that I remembered from my childhood)—much longer than we had intended. Most of the time was spent talking to Lall, whose knowledge of the history of the islands was encyclopaedic. He confirmed the impression I had gained from my grandfather's books that the so-called friendly tribes—those that had had most contact with outsiders, the so called Great Andamanese—had died off the soonest while the hostile Jarawa and Onge—those that had scrupulously avoided contact—had lasted the longest. I had yet to appreciate how wrong Grandfather was when he postulated that it was the unfriendly Jarawa, who in his days still existed in viable numbers, who were in the greatest danger because of their refusal to cooperate with the authorities.

Lall threw light on another bit of history which I had found puzzling, the so called Andaman Homes that had been set up by the British to feed and nurture the islanders while developing some mutual understanding. The British had meant them as a point of contact—and not of control, as suggested by the historian Clare Anderson—but their purpose had been turned on its head by the spread of disease and by malpractice. This outcome was unintended, though it reflected a lack of supervision and could have been foreseen, since control of the homes had been given to the rough-and-ready Naval Brigade. It was through the brigade in particular, and through the convicts who were co-opted to provide the agricultural labour, that syphilis was spread to the tribes. Deaths from this disease were very numerous and were compounded by sufferers being put to death by their fellow tribespeople, who had no idea of where the disease had come from and merely wanted to prevent it spreading.

Lall told us that due to increasing contact with settlers, the Onge on Little Andaman were now down to about a hundred and that thanks to the ATR and tourism, the Jarawa were becoming increasingly dependent. Their three main communities now numbered about 500 with one community, the Tirrur people, particularly determined to maintain their traditional isolation. Lall also said that the name 'Jarawa' did not denote a separate tribe but was a name given to any 'others' or 'outsiders'—those who are not 'us'; thus the inhabitants of North Sentinel Island were still sometimes referred to as Jarawa by inhabitants of other islands. He told me that he believed that for them more than any other tribespeople, there was hope of longer term survival, but that nobody knew whether there were as few as fifty or as many as 200 people on the island. He also said that aerial observations never detected females, probably because the approach of aircraft prompted the men to hide the women away for fear that they might be captured.

The other prominent member of the Local Born Society we met was John Lobo, in his little flat in downtown Port Blair. John too spoke freely. He is of mixed Indian, Portuguese and British extraction and, like Denis and Lall, speaks passionately about his hopes for the future of the tribes and his love of the Andamans. He was born in 1930 and was a teenager during the Japanese occupation and says that during that time they killed over 3,000 settlers whom they considered hostile. In general the Japanese did not interfere with the tribes, however, though they carried out some indiscriminate bombing against the Jarawa, whom they suspected of cooperating with the British.

John said that, like many other people, he had little idea what the government thought about the Jarawa and their future. There did not seem to be a coherent policy. He thought tribal land was being encroached on and said that many settlers felt they ought to be custodians, with special responsibilities towards the tribes. It was a theme about which he had written a lot and was one of the reasons why he had campaigned for Andaman independence.

After John had shown us more old photographs of Local Born Society members, including another of Uncle Roo, we went back to the hotel. I telephoned to try and get an appointment with the chief of police, to discuss the police's role in preventing settler and tourist encroachment on to Jarawa land. Sadly the police could not agree to a meeting.

Instead Juliet and I went to call on the deputy commissioner or DC, the administrator responsible for about a third of the archipelago including Port Blair. His secretary regretted that we would have to wait for about half an hour so to fill the time we asked to see the archive records of Grandfather, George Anson and Uncle Roo, which I had been told were kept in the offices. The secretary sent us to the Archive Office which was nearby, only to be told when we got there that nothing could be shown to us without the DC's specific, written authority. I suppose we have only ourselves to blame for exporting bureaucracy to the empire.

The DC when we saw him was young and impressive and a member of the IAS (Indian Administrative Service), the successor to the ICS of my grandfather's day. His appointment, made by central government, reflects the fact that the Andamans are governed directly by Delhi and not by a devolved authority. In the opinion of many islanders this means that officials seldom spend enough time in the islands to understand the full complexity of local problems. At the same time a lack of accountability and a distance from higher echelons enables administrators to take important decisions without fear of being questioned. This seems to have happened over the Indian Supreme Court's order to close the ATR which has never been complied with. It also seems to have happened over a permit issued in Delhi to the scientist Erika Hagelberg to visit the Onge tribe to collect DNA, which was then ignored by local officialdom and police.

The DC came across as open minded. While he acknowledged that policy on the division of land between the settlers and the tribes lacked clarity, he said that the embargo of 2002 on settler encroachment on the tribal land had been upheld.

After that day's meetings, there was an opportunity to talk to Denis Giles again when he brought Ambika, the trainee journalist, from the mainland to interview me for the *Andaman Chronicle*. He said that all the British wanted from the Andamans in 1857 was to establish a penal colony and nothing more. The convicts imprisoned there were not freedom fighters, as modern historians now habitually portray them, but it was they who brought modernity to the islands. He said that the Great Andamanese of mainly Middle and North Andaman were in fact nine different tribes who remained separate and often mutually hostile. The names of all these tribes began with *Aka*. The alternative names of the other two tribes, the Jarawa and the Onge, began with *Ang* meaning outsiders. The Aka tribes were all now close to extinction. It was they who had had the closest contact with non-Andamanese in Grandfather's day, including trading relations with the British. Today, the numbers of Jarawa mainly on South Andaman and Onge on Little Andaman where they lived adjacent to settlers were holding up well.

Denis accepted that contact between settlers and tourists was destructive to the tribespeople but felt one had to try to be optimistic about their prospects.

On Friday, our fifth full day, the faithful Aziz drove us to the harbour where with a hundred or so other passengers, we boarded a large motorized catamaran for the two-hour voyage eastward to Havelock Island. Here entrepreneurs have been allowed to build hotels on an island forty miles square where there are now settlers but no longer any native Andamanese. Havelock's potential to attract tourists was highlighted in an article in the *Sunday Telegraph* which I had read shortly before embarking on our Andaman expedition. It described a beach[5] on the island as one of the most serene and pristine in Asia. Bordering on it were two excellent hotels. We were booked into the one buried in dense jungle only few hundred yards inland, the 'Barefoot'. 'Here,' according to the hotel's publicity, 'you experience the uncharted, the raw wilderness of untouched forests that stretch till the sparkling ocean' and it was precisely that forest habitat of which I wanted to get a better sense.

Havelock harbour was teeming with tourists and day visitors. We hailed a tuk tuk and were driven along a winding, narrow tar road past settlers' houses around which the forest had been cleared and bananas, betel nut palms and other crops had been planted. Space was not a problem, and for mile after mile we found houses that were sometimes alongside the road and sometimes a distance away. There seemed to have been no planning. Gradually the signs of human habitation became fewer until after ten miles we turned into a patch of thick forest. There in a clearing was the Barefoot.

Though I had expected it to be more or less on the beach, I was not disappointed. It was set among some of the biggest trees I have ever seen and which towered over a thatched wooden building with reception lounge and bar. It was an area you were only allowed into after removing your shoes. Facing it across a small lawn was an open-sided dining room. The buildings, furniture and decoration were what the brochure called 'island-inspired' with 'tents, cottages and villas … constructed using renewable materials such as cane, thatch, and wood', making it 'the only ecologically friendly resort in the Andamans'. Beyond the dining room, a narrow path led through an undergrowth of smaller trees, all struggling upward to reach the light, to our two-storey hut buried in the jungle, out of sight.

After dropping our luggage we made our way to the beach, breaking through the green wall of trees. The beach was indeed long and beautiful with surf pounding on the reef beyond the white of the coral sand. There were very few people around and we decided to walk the half mile or so to another hotel, the Taj Exotica, which was also much lauded by the *Sunday Telegraph*. It was evening and we thought we might stay for a drink. No luck. The guards on the gate

5 Radhanagar Beach, 'Travel Inspiration', *Sunday Telegraph*, 31 December 2017.

Forest meets beach on Havelock Island: 'some of the biggest trees I have ever seen'.

beside the beach would not let us in. In any case they said the hotel did not sell alcohol. We were not too disappointed as, unlike the Barefoot, the hotel's more modern buildings seemed less in keeping with the environment. We made our way back to the Barefoot's bar, open on all sides to the forest, to enjoy our evening drinks in the company of a truly international clientele. Over dinner we were serenaded by owls—probably the Andaman hawk owl, we were told. We could easily have been in the deepest jungle of the Congo.

The next morning we awoke to unfamiliar but beautiful birdsong and after breakfast explored the resort gardens and surrounds. We became aware of the great variety of birds, only one of which we knew. Many were in the high canopy but I saw a local parakeet and a visitor from the mainland—a red-whiskered bulbul —with which I had become familiar in Mauritius. We also heard the tapping of woodpeckers and imagined local species such as the exotic olive-backed sunbird and the blue-tailed bee-eater.

We wanted to explore so we arranged for the hotel taxi to take us to another hotel some way inland. So it was back down the road towards the port and inland up into the hills. I had expected to find ourselves in forest but we were disappointed. Though the hotel had charm, it looked over neighbouring settler properties with their alien bananas and coconuts, so we returned to the outstanding Barefoot, the forest location of which, together with its outstanding service and comfort, put it in the highest category.

Here, for the first time on our trip, we came across Western tourists. The couples, one each from Germany, Italy and Spain, were as enthusiastic about the place as we were. I was left with the feeling that the Barefoot can teach the Andaman authorities a number of lessons in how to develop an international tourist industry. The Indian government apparently does not currently favour such an expansion. I am happy with that. Until the ATR has been shut down, there should be no expansion, for the sake of the Jarawa. After that, there is an abundance of untouched islands on which a newly focused tourist industry could develop.

Next day we joined the crowds at Havelock port for the return voyage to Port Blair and the drive to the airport with Aziz. Due to cloud cover there were no views of North Sentinel this time but there were compensations: Chennai airport was modern and efficient; Mumbai airport—by the architectural practice SOM—was modern and huge, and one of the most architecturally stunning I have seen. And so we flew home. Overall I think Juliet and I had made a pretty good team.

Our adventure had been stimulating and enjoyable and helped to make a lot more sense of the impressions I had gained from Granny and Grandfather's writings, and those of Mary, and what my mother had told me. I was also starting to read the book by the Indian physician, Dr Kar, whose experience of the Jarawa over recent years is unmatched and may never be repeated.

I had always feared that I might be disappointed if I visited India, of which I have so many wonderful childhood memories. In the event the Andamans had been a delight, with friendly people who share with India the values of democracy, free speech and the rule of law that have made it a global success story. I left the region with my lifelong attachment to the country renewed, with feelings of great pride in the role that Britain has played in this, and my determination to write the story of the Andaman Islands reinforced. Everybody Juliet and I met had been incredibly friendly and welcoming. Time and again we were asked to pose with friendly Indian fellow tourists all interested to hear of our family connection with the islands. They treated us like Andamanian celebrities. I had not expected that.

Chapter 8

Family and Empire

My family's centuries-old involvement with India came to an end in 1947. Just before the sub-continent gained its independence, my parents, sister Veronica and brother Roger travelled to Peshawar, capital of the North-West Frontier Province, en route to Bombay (Mumbai) from where we would sail away on a 19,000-ton Cunader, the *Scythia*, which had been converted to a troopship.

We spent one memorable night in Peshawar, staying with the governor Sir Olaf Caroe and his wife in Government House. I recall about supper time Sir Olaf telling me he had received a message that there were two boys on bicycles at the main gate who wanted to see me. I ran across the lawn and there among the throng of supplicants waiting to petition him were my very good friends David and Roger Ahmed who had come to say goodbye. We went on to correspond for many years.

The train journey from Peshawar to Bombay took two days. When we got there, the atmosphere was somehow festive. The part of the city where we were put up was full of British people enjoying themselves before their final departure, with people from Peshawar staying at the British club at Marvi. At Beach Kandy up the coast I enjoyed my very first swim in the sea and, for the last time before we left India for ever, saw friends from our wonderful boarding school in Kashmir.

In Bombay, while waiting for our ship, we stayed for three or four days with a family friend, a bachelor with a grand flat on Back Bay. My mother had proudly taken us to see the magnificent monument near the harbour, the so-called 'Gateway of India', and we paid my first-ever visit to a Chinese restaurant, where I decided that I had never tasted such delicious food in my life. It was fun for all of us, this prelude to the coming sadness. I listened jealously to Mum's account of the grown-ups' visit to the cinema to see a musical that had just been released. We were so pre-occupied that

Soldiers of the British Indian Army parade in front of Government House.

there was no time to reflect on what it meant to be leaving wonderful India for the last time.

Our family connection with India went back to the days of the East India Company, which had been granted a royal charter to trade in the East Indies by Elizabeth I in 1600 and which went on to govern India and control half the world's trade before its administrative and military operations were subsumed by Britain in 1858 and finally wound up in 1874. Reginald Lowis's father Edmund had been commissioner of several Indian provinces before retiring to the English West Country in 1891. His grandfather John, born in 1823, had also been in the ICS. Bessie Coldstream was the daughter of William Coldstream ICS, whose Indian connections went back generations, and the beautiful Fanny Anson, sister of Sir George Anson, who had been military superintendent in the Andamans. The Ansons too had the strongest Indian connections, most of them military. Their father had commanded the Indian Army at the time of the Indian Mutiny.

Reginald and Bessie married in England in 1901. The national census of that year records that Bessie's brother John was at the time staying with Reggie's father Edmund Lowis in the West Country. No doubt he was checking out the Lowises on behalf of the Coldstreams as a whole. John went on to become chief justice of the Punjab—another crucial connection.

Reggie was born in India in 1867. As was customary in those days among children of British civil servants in India, he was sent to school in England. Years went by without his seeing his parents and having to spend his holidays with relatives. The only account of his early childhood comes from my mother who, in her memoir of her father, wrote up two anecdotes that became family legend.

The first is inconsequential: as a carriage that was taking Reggie to his prep school set off, his great friend 'Buttons' (because his uniform was ornamented with a fine set of crested buttons) ran out of the house to present a button to Reggie to add to his already formidable collection. The second is more significant. During the summer of 1882, Reggie and his three sisters and four brothers were staying with relations and spent time with neighbours, the Wolseleys— Lieutenant General Sir Garnet, later Lord Wolseley. One day in September, as the children were rampaging around the house, Lady Wolseley came to the top of the stairs, reading a letter, with tears streaming down her face. She singled him out, calling 'come here Reggie,' and as he stood huffing and puffing downstairs she said, 'You will always remember this day, Reggie; my husband has won a great victory!' It was the battle of Tel el Kabir, in which the British army managed to secure the Suez Canal from attack by the Egyptian army.

My mother went on to write about Reggie's time at Sherborne where, he told her, he was incapable of doing a stroke of work, like many members of the family including herself. Many years later she wrote that when asked to explain my lack of application in the classroom by my headmaster in South Africa, she replied 'Oh, it's hereditary; I was the same', and added, 'We all turn into quite hard-working men and women.'

Reggie was sent to Heidelberg University in Germany to study forestry. There he lived with a local family, became fluent in German and developed a great love for the German people. He also fell wildly and deeply in love with the 14-year-old daughter of the family. They wanted to marry but the grown-ups disapproved. He never forgot her.

After Heidelberg Reggie was accepted into the Indian Forestry Service and spent the next ten years in various parts of the sub-continent, including Burma. It was from there that he was sent to the Andamans and met Bessie. As in Heidelberg the prospective marriage did not at first attract universal approval from the Anson and Coldstream families because RFL, as my mother called him, had little money and few prospects, but he made a good impression and people tended to like him from the start. He had charm and it became increasingly apparent that more than anything else he was what is now called a 'people person'.

RFL was now 34 and in terms of his career, it was his relative maturity, by ICS standards, combined with his familiarity with the prevailing culture and way of life in imperial India and Burma that worked most in his favour. Following his return to the Andamans from England as a married man, with Bessie, in 1901, he threw himself into the many and varied responsibilities of his new administrative job. This included the care of the convicts, the indigenous people and the forestry industry as well as a personal interest in natural history, which included research into a local anopheles mosquito which my mother records as being named after him in 1910—the *aedimorphus lowisii*—by the mosquito cataloguer F.V. Theobald (of special interest in view of the immunity enjoyed by Andamanese aboriginals against malaria).

Reginald on his yacht: gave access to the Andamans and Nicobars' 572 islands.

Reginald's diversity and his emphasis on people skills made him entirely suitable for his new responsibilities and his promotion to assistant commissioner. As noted earlier, he was fully involved from the start with the progressive new approach towards the rehabilitation of the convicts and was committed to the well-being of the indigenous tribes.

In her memoir my mother describes family life on Viper Island in the Port Blair harbour, where the Lowises had their house. She talks about how she and her sister Janet were cared for by a British nanny and lived on a sparse diet, as her mother believed in giving children only the simplest food. As was customary, Nanny played a major role in the children's upbringing and they had minimal contact with their parents, and Mum writes of her mother's groans at the prospect of having to give the children tea on Nanny's day off.

By contrast, Reggie, her father, lightened Bessie's burden with stories that he made up as he went along. When once she had earache he put her on his shoulder and walked her up and down the long verandah reciting Edward Lear and especially 'The Pobble who has no Toes'. She writes also of her deep contentment with her face against his shoulder, damp with his sweat and her tears.

Mum described her father as a very compassionate man, capable of great rages 'but always for the right reasons'. When she was very small, she says, she told her father how she had pulled the legs off a fly to see if it could escape without them. He was furious and smacked her, asking her how she would like it if someone did that to her? She said it gave her an indelible lesson on what was fair. Another of Mum's Andaman memories describes how, when the family was

Elizabeth and Janet Lowis with their mother Bessie: they had 'minimal contact'.

bowling along in a rickshaw, they saw a large group of toadstools growing beside the road. They were white, green, yellow and orange and as the family stopped to look at them, RFL told the children never to touch them. Many years later Mum asked her father if there were luminous toadstools in the Andamans. He said there were but that they were very rare, and added that the family had once seen a splendid group of them. 'I know,' said my mother; 'it was on my fourth birthday' and she described the colours exactly.

Mum remembered the death of Reginald's dog Paddy, an Irish terrier. 'RFL adored it,' she wrote. 'He came into our room rather late one night. Janet had gone to sleep but I sat up and said "How's Paddy?" And I can still see the grief on his face as I pressed my face into his starched shirt and soaked it with my tears. He tried to cheer me up and said, "Now look what you've done to my lovely clean shirt front," which of course made me laugh.'

In 1911 the Lowis family returned to England and stayed with relations while Mum and Janet started school. Mum remembered her headmistress talking repeatedly about the threat posed by the growing size of the German army and her father, always an optimist, pooh-poohing the idea of German bellicosity but agreeing that Britain would be unprepared, should war break out. When my grandparents' leave ran out and they returned to the Andamans, Mum and Janet stayed on, which meant not seeing their parents for the next four years. Mum writes that she had no memory of feeling homesick. On the contrary, she says, school was a relief from the nursery and from Nanny, who dominated their life in the Andamans. She remembered being exceptionally naughty while Janet was always good; at some point Janet still had no bad marks whereas Mum had accumulated thirty.

Back in the Andamans the two younger children, Mary and John, were being brought up in the family home on Viper Island. My mother tells of how she overheard Bessie confiding to friends that whereas she had been very strict with her elder two, she was determined to enjoy the company of Mary and John. The result, Mum said, was that they were 'spoiled rotten', something Mum deeply resented. At the same time she acknowledged that Mary at eight was much more sophisticated than she had been at thirteen and Janet at eleven-and-a-half.

Meanwhile Lowis, as the seemingly permanent fixture in the Andamans Commission, was gaining unrivalled experience.

Mary and John Lowis with their father: more indulged than Elizabeth and Janet.

Following his work in supervising the 1911 census he continued to travel widely around the islands, including the Nicobars, and strengthened a growing reputation for administrative excellence, for cultivating friendly relations with the Great Andamanese and for building tentative links with the other tribes as well. Although British policy had always been to leave what were then twelve tribes to their own devices, it seemed reasonable to most observers that efforts to understand them and get to know them better would not go amiss. My mother had strong memories of visits to the Onge tribe on Little Andaman and Rutland Island and with the Great Andamanese on Middle and North Andaman, and tribal children

'Heart-warming: a canoe bearing a gift of dugong tusks for my grandparents.'

were welcomed to Government House on Ross Island. A heart-warming tribal response came with the arrival of a two-person canoe bearing a gift of dugong tusks for my grandparents. A reciprocal visit of this sort was unprecedented.

A highlight of the period just before the First World War was a visit to the home of a well-known marine biologist who sparked a new family interest in the unrivalled, rich environment of coral and of every tropical sea creature it is possible to imagine. There was also a visit from a delightful Anson cousin, Maudie, then still in her teens, who brought joy and laughter to the Lowis family. Meanwhile RFL gained promotion to deputy commissioner and started to spend long periods as acting commissioner when the family moved into Government House on Ross Island. It was there that he gained the nickname 'Admiral of the Port'.

He and Bessie returned to England with Mary and John in 1916 while the First World War was in full swing. Now the family could be together again and a new era started when they were offered Bessie's brother's house near Maidenhead, on the river Thames. Mum's memory of the Maidenhead house was of food shortages leading to a diet of mostly potato cakes fried in what she describes as 'filthy stuff called cocoa butter'. To compensate there was a wonderful library where she says her longing to read and learn poetry was made possible by 'those lovely stuffed bookshelves'. She remembers Maidenhead too for her father's introduction to what was to become his greatest pleasure, the soil. At first the gardener looked at Reggie's efforts at digging with pity and said it looked as if a pig had been rooting there. He soon became an expert, however, and the family came to enjoy an enormously improved diet with all sorts of vegetables.

After leave, RFL returned to India alone and this time, Mum says, the parting was very different, with Bessie missing him dreadfully. At that point she and the children moved into lodgings in London. The family had been experiencing financial hardships, when suddenly their circumstances changed. Bessie's aunt died and the family moved into Binfield Priory in Berkshire, an early eighteenth-century rectory, extended in the 1820s and now listed Grade II.

With all the children settled in boarding schools, Bessie went back to the Andamans after the war to join RFL. Despite his wide responsibilities, he took on responsibility for the next census. Again there was no cooperation from the Jarawa and only estimates of their number were possible. This may reflect the failure of the British to court them. Since the census of 1911 no further visits had been paid to Rutland Island, and only a few to Little Andaman, where the semi-friendly Onge had underlined their basic tribal attitude to outsiders by killing members of the crew of a Chinese ship which had made the fatal mistake of going ashore.

In 1922 came Reginald's retirement and he and Bessie moved to Canada where he thrived on the egalitarian culture where everyone knew each other by their Christian names. After all the protocol of high office, my mother said that he enjoyed the new lack of formality. It was a difficult time however for Bessie who throughout her life had never done any physical housework. No doubt this was one of the reasons why before long the Lowises left Canada and settled back in Binfield Priory.

My mother, who by now had left school and was visiting her parents in Binfield for the first time, remembers her father's physical strength, enhanced by all his gardening. She was at once put to work weeding, apparently because she knew all the wild flowers and could distinguish them from the cultivars, but also perhaps so that Reggie could monopolize her company. It was in the garden that she and her father did most of their talking, leaving Bessie unattended. Bessie resented this, as she did the thought of Mum sitting talking over dinner to Reggie if she was in bed, where she often sought sanctuary when feeling rejected. Mum wrote, however, that she longed to know more about her father's experiences in the Andamans and felt there were great gaps in her knowledge.

My mother enjoyed another opportunity to be on her own with my grandfather in 1926 when an Indian friend living in London, a

Elizabeth and Reginald Lowis: 'left Canada and settled back in Binfield Priory'.

scholar and mathematician, approached RFL with a new gambling system that he had devised. The friend wanted someone he trusted to go to Monte Carlo, try out the system, keep careful notes and come back to him with the results. RFL jumped at the chance. While he and Elizabeth stayed at a pension in Nice, he divided his time between exploring the Indian scholar's theories in the gambling rooms and swimming and exploring the coast with his daughter. The highlight of the trip was an unforgettable few days walking in the Maritime Alps, with Mum carrying only a rucksack bearing a spare pair of knickers, a toothbrush, a jersey, brushes and paints and a tin for wild flowers. In her memoir Mum describes the delight of staying in little peasant farm houses, eating slabs of goat meat for lunch and the simplest cuisine in the evening, painting the wild flowers that she'd picked and being chased by local border police suspicious of what the couple were up to along the wild mountainous frontier between France and Italy.

Before going to the Riviera, my mother had completed a teacher's training course and then spent a year teaching in Jamaica. It was a happy and formative time for her. She loved the Jamaicans and developed an antipathy towards any kind of racism, a quality that stood her in good stead when she returned to India in 1931 and shaped her contempt for the white behaviour that she encountered later in southern Africa. Before returning to India she spent a couple of years in the English Lake District tutoring Betty (Elizabeth), the elder daughter of a prominent Lake District family, the Lofties, and helping her get into Oxford.

The Lofties became lifelong friends and the mother, Madeleine, became my godmother. While in the Lakes, my mother acquired a love of climbing that she would develop on her return to India.

Mum was drawn back to India by generations of family tradition and by her childhood experiences, just as her parents had been. She headed for Lahore where John Coldstream, her uncle, was chief justice of the Punjab and got a job in a girls' boarding school. There she combined work with an active social life, sometimes having to climb over the surrounding wall to get back into school after lights out.

In those days, I remember her saying, there was a serious shortage of eligible males to marry or even socialize with because so many had been killed during the First World War. Mum was adventurous and self-sufficient, however, and soon sought out my father.

Wilfred, known as Pip, was a civil engineer in the Indian Service of Engineers in Lahore, five years out of Imperial College, London. One of his attractions was that his work took him frequently into remote rural areas where he lived a life of shooting, fishing and camping beside the mighty River Indus. It was a life he was happy to share with Mum and which she adored. She made him promise that their expeditions would continue if she married him. He rashly agreed and they married—but within weeks he was transferred to the North West Frontier Province, where in 1936 I was born in Murree in the Galyat region of the Pir Panjal mountain range.

Our family's ties with India and the Andamans were strengthened when my mother's sister Mary returned with Roo Deane, whom she had married in England in 1930, as previously noted. Roo's posting the same year as assistant commissioner of police to the Andaman Islands was ideal for them, so idyllic had her childhood years there been. Roo was also able to capitalize on the affection in which Reggie was still held by those who remembered him. Both their children, Shirley and Tim, were born in the little hospital on Ross Island, as Mary had been. The Deanes' four years on the islands went very well and Roo distinguished himself.

Mary, who at the age of five, had been photographed meeting a group of two dozen naked Andamanese males who looked at her in understandable uncertainty, went on in her old age to broadcast her Andaman memories on the BBC (*see pages 84–85 and Appendix 6*). Roo became superintendent of police in Amritsar. As described in Larry Collins and Dominique Lapierre's 1975 book *Freedom at Midnight*, about the British handover of power to India in 1947, Roo tried to calm down the ethnic violence between Hindus and Sikhs by getting the police band to play Gilbert and Sullivan favourites in Amritsar's central square.[6] Following retirement he became director of the Pakistan Service of the BBC and both he and Mary were stalwarts of the Pakistan Society.

My father Wilfred, born in Yorkshire, had worked extraordinarily hard to get grants and scholarships to help him up the educational ladder. He was a keen sportsman and was the mile and half-mile champion at Imperial College, where he read engineering. In India, which he adapted to enthusiastically, he excelled in tennis, golf and polo. He was also a keen shot and many were the shoots for *chikor*

---

[6] Deane is wrongly named 'Rule' in the book.

(the local dry land partridge), in the low hills on the Afghan border, and for duck and snipe in the marsh lands beside the Indus and its tributaries.

I have the strongest memories of Dad teaching me to fish when I was eight, on a family trip up the Kaghan Valley in what is now the Mansehra District of the Khyber Pakhtunkhwa province of Pakistan, leading up to the high Himalayas. We walked or rode on donkeys and stayed in a series of rest houses or *dak bungalows* higher and higher up the valley. He caught innumerable trout. Under his instruction I dragged a silver spoon attached to a length of bamboo through the water and was suddenly taken by a fair-sized fish. Before proudly delivering my catch to Mum I remember running down the river bank to an elderly Indian couple who lived in a little stone house above the water to boast about it. They invited me in and gave me a piece of delicious *chapati*, unusually made of maize meal, which accompanied their evening meal.

My father's career in India was very successful. He learned Pashtu, had several promotions to get the top job in the North West Frontier Province, and was awarded the OBE. Before leaving India at independence he was offered the job of Chief Engineer in Bengal but declined the offer because he and my mother foresaw problems over the education of us children.

My own abiding memories of India are of two homes, both in Khyber Pakhtunkhwa: one in the mountains in the summer capital Nathia Gali, the other in the hot plains of Bannu, the frontier town right on the border of tribal territory between what was then India and Afghanistan where the British had been fighting off Pashtun skirmishes for generations. When Dad and other civil servants had to go from Bannu into the tribal badlands of Waziristan, on the border between the North West Frontier Province of India and Afghanistan, they travelled with two Waziri bodyguards called, as I remember, '*bedruggers*' who squatted facing each other in the back of the station wagon with rifles slung across their shoulders. The advantage of employing them in this way was that it acted as a deterrent to the constant danger of kidnapping, because if harm came to a bodyguard this risked triggering a blood feud which nobody wanted.

A dramatic moment I remember in Bannu took place when a military friend based in tribal territory called on us. He was enjoying a drink with my parents on the lawn when I spotted that he

Mary Lowis, photographed by Henry W. Seton-Karr in 1911, greeting islanders.

The author in July 1939, a month before his 3rd birthday, with his father Wilfred.

had left his service revolver on the front seat of his Land Rover. I picked it up, cocked it, pointed it at the ground and pulled the trigger. There was a big bang, a hole appeared in the drive and I stood shocked as visitor and parents came running across the lawn towards me.

Inside the Bannu cantonment, with its city and fort, founded in 1848 by Sir Herbert Edwardes, I was free to wander anywhere and everywhere. Unlike the coddled sons of the district commissioner, I enjoyed the closest contact with the locals, spoke their language fluently and socialized with them in the city and the bazaar and played with their children. I specially remember the Gurkha guards at the entrance of the great Bannu fort with its high sloping mud walls and how they taught me and the brigadier's son how to blow a bugle.

In Nathia I enjoyed similar freedom in a beautiful hill station set in the pine and fir trees 9,000 feet up in the mountains. From the wind in the trees came a sound like the sea. In the woods grew the tiny Himalayan strawberries of which we never tired eating. In between adventures, my friend Dougal, son of the officer commanding the training school for Ghurka recruits, climbed the mountains with the young men proudly wearing the smaller size traditional *kukri* army knives, with which we had been presented by Dougal's father, around our waists.

At other times there were lessons when Mum taught sister Veronica and me Latin and read us Kipling, Dickens, Andrew Lang's *Tales of Troy and Greece* and Henrietta Elizabeth Marshall's *Our Island Story* and we learned Tennyson's 'The Revenge' by heart:

> And they stared at the dead that had been so valiant and true,
> And had holden the power and glory of Spain so cheap
> That he dared her with one little ship and his English few ...

In the summer of 1944 I was sent to a boarding school in Kashmir for British boys who but for the war would have been sent home to England. There, under the inspired headmastership of Eric Tyndale-Biscoe (known as TB), son of the missionary Cecil, known as the founder of modern Kashmir, I immediately bought into everything TB and the school stood for and had to offer.

Though I missed home I was happy from the start. The Tyndale-Biscoes' priority was not converting the locals to Christianity but influencing them in ways that would help them to help their fellow men. Thus in this land of lakes they were taught to swim so they could save their neighbours from drowning, and to box and be fit so they could defend themselves and their values. It was all about caring for your fellow and standing up for what was good, right and true. These were the values to which we were encouraged to aspire at the school called Sheikh Bagh in Srinagar.

Along the way there was no room for racism and though the majority of boys were British from all over India, the school had a healthy number of Indian boys, sons of local business people, some from as far away as Karachi or Delhi.

Thanks to my mother's teaching I found the lessons easy. Otherwise we spent days on end swimming and boating in the Dal Lake, camping beside the mighty Wular Lake, climbing the 13,003-feet Mahadeo Peak and skiing in the hill station of Gulmarg. We aspired to physical and mental toughness. Our school motto was 'In all things be men.'

For me the influence of Sheikh Bagh, which affected the rest of my life and particularly my time in Africa, was the way I came to see race, something I am sure that all of us Sheikh Bagh boys shared. After that experience, a smart English prep school seemed to stand for nothing. It was particularly the influence of Sheikh Bagh which impressed me about the Indian Civil Service, which cultivated a relationship of mutual respect with the locals, led me to feel so disgusted by the racism I encountered in southern Africa in later years and was a major influence on my decision to seek entrance into Her Majesty's Overseas Civil Service.

On arriving in England just before Indian independence in 1947 we had gone straight to my Lowis grandparents Reggie and Bessie, who had now downsized from Binfield Priory and installed themselves in Lavender Cottage, also near Bracknell in Berkshire. It was the first time I had met them. I thought Grandfather was wonderful (Mum said he disliked being called Grandpa), fit and physical in his large and beautiful garden. Bessie was sweet, old and slow-moving. In her memoir of her father Mum says that Bessie disapproved of me because of my tendency to answer back but adds that I was never rude. Grandfather, she said, entirely approved of the 'violent' sense of independence shown by me and my younger brother Roger, and added that I met him on 'a man-to-man' basis. I remember him as the kindest, gentlest man—a grown-up I could really talk to. We practised throwing and catching a cricket ball,

The author in Bannu, 1943, with his mother and sister Veronica: 'independent'.

though it bruised his hands. He told us children's stories about family excursions to Andamanese islands and taught us songs including a children's hymn he had composed which ended with the words 'they must wash behind their ears'.

Even in those days I was interested in international affairs and Grandfather and our talks about India and the role of the British Empire across the world caught my imagination. I learned later that before Indian independence he had written to the British foreign secretary to suggest that Britain should establish a naval base on the Andamans. We became real friends and he was happy to lend me his bicycle, though I could barely reach the pedals. I was allowed to go off on long bike rides by myself around the Berkshire country-side, something else of which Bessie disapproved, my mother said.

In spite of that, my main memory of Bessie was of her great kindness. I had taken to reading a particular comic, *The Champion*, with adventure stories about heroes like the Spitfire pilot and boxer Rockfist Rogan with which she approved and which she started to send me at prep school. Unfortunately my miserable school banned comics and I was obliged to ask her to stop sending them.

I spent a year and a half at that dreadful institution, without seeing my parents. Dad went directly to Southern Rhodesia from India and Mum, Veronica and Roger joined him there. I missed India and found nobody at all, child or grown up, which whom I could share my feelings of deep loss. A master at the school wanted me to stay with him one holiday. I smelt a rat and had I been bigger might have flattened him with a right cross, as advocated by TB at Sheikh Bagh.

In 1948 I left Britain for southern Africa and was sent to boarding schools in Southern Rhodesia and South Africa. I did not return for 11 years, by which time I had still not had a real conversation with a black man. Neither had I got to know what I came to see as the real Africa. Nevertheless I had loved Rhodes University, in Grahamstown, Eastern Cape Province, where my main subject was French and where the standard achieved in those days was far higher in both fluency in the language and in literature than at Cambridge, where I was about to start a one-year course, prior to joining the Colonial Service.

I soon went down to see RFL who, following Granny's death, had moved into a flat in a large house called Hollybank. He was now 93, bright as a button, as interested as ever in what was going on in the world, including Africa, and doing the Times crossword puzzle every day. He was delighted that I was joining the Colonial Service. He was worried, though, about the situation in Southern Rhodesia and shared my view that Britain could be doing much more in the region to steer it away from racism and the extremes of both white and black nationalism.

He seemed touchingly moved and pleased when I travelled down to see him with a Cambridge girlfriend, just before sailing for Africa. He came into his own again a year later at my sister Veronica's wedding, which was held in the garden at Hollybank. He emerged for the ceremony in full regalia of morning suit, including spats, and everyone wanted to talk to him. Sadly I missed the event as I had started work as a cadet in Northern Rhodesia. Shortly after this I received a telegram to say that he had died. My parents saw the announcement in a copy of the Times as they were travelling down the Suez Canal on their way back to Southern Rhodesia.

In her memoir my mother wondered whether she had painted a clear enough picture of her father. Had she caught his sparkle? Had she been too detailed and lacked perspective? Reflecting on those of her father's qualities that appealed to her most, she mentioned his detachment. She said that he never interfered and never fretted about our souls—in fact he was not greatly concerned with them —'but minded a lot about our minds, bodies, happiness and bank balances'. He was neither humble nor conceited, she felt, but balanced.

I saw him as open-minded, loyal, straight and entirely lacking in the arrogance one might have associated with his job and status. He never took himself seriously nor did he seek to dominate. When Bessie was alive RFL's life was clearly dedicated to her. Despite the long periods that he and my mother had lived on different continents, his influence on her was also undiminished, in spite of their not seeing each other.

I wish I could say that my grandfather also had a personal relationship with the indigenous Andamanese people, but it was never possible for him to have any such communication, any more than it was for Radcliffe-Brown or T.N. Pandit or E.H. Man. This frustrates me enormously in some ways but also helps me appreciate how detached we are. Only Dr. Kar ever got really close —but that is part of why this story is so special.

At the start of the 20th century The Andaman and Nicobar Islands, which stretch north–south for 600 miles in the Bay of Bengal, were virtually unknown to the world. The Andamans—the 242 northern islands—are volcanic in origin and covered with almost impregnable tropical forest made up of hundreds of endemic species growing in the rich soil, made up largely of ash. To the south, the Nicobar Islands are populated by people of mixed oriental origins, who have always enjoyed trading relations with the outside world.

The principal Andamans land mass consists of three islands of similar size running north–south in close proximity. All were populated by aboriginal tribes, with the nine so called Great Andamanese tribes on North and Middle Andaman and the Jarawa on South Andaman. On the southern tip of the latter is Port Blair. Further south and nearby is Rutland Island, populated by a few Onge people. Rutland used to have a population of Jarawa but they moved to South Andaman in the early 1900s. Further south still is Little Andaman where lives most of the Onge tribe. Forty miles to the west of Port Blair is North Sentinel, home of the notorious Sentinelese.

The only sizeable mammals on the Andamans, all hunted by the islanders, are dugong, found mainly among the widespread mangroves, a species of wild pig and a fruit-eating civet cat. Birds, including several endemic species, are abundant but because they mostly live high in the tree canopy are not hunted, for fear of wasting valuable arrows.

As far back as anyone has ever known, the Andamans have been populated by tribes of so-called Negrito people who, armed with bows and arrows, gained a fearsome reputation for killing anyone who came near them. This reputation, including rumours of cannibalism, kept the world away so that even though Denmark formally annexed the islands in the mid-1700s, it quickly lost interest in them.

The aboriginal hostility of which Captain Blair soon became aware arose from deep instinct reinforced by brushes with slavers and with Arab and Portuguese navigators. Marco Polo described them as having heads, eyes and teeth like dogs. They were not cannibals, however, as he asserted, though what he wrote about them around 1300 encouraged Blair to write them off nearly five centuries later as being the lowest possible form of humanity. The natives, Blair wrote, were 'crafty, vengeful and brutish' and 'in respect of their manners they are of the lowest yet to be discovered in the scale of civilization—man in the rudest state of nature'. Avoidance of all contact meant their inability to learn and develop, except in one respect: while hostile to the outside world, they evidently welcomed shipwrecks as their only source of metal from which to fashion tips for deadly arrows and spears.

The brief period of British interest in the islands begins with the survey carried out between December 1788 and April 1789 by Captain Archibald Blair for the British Government with a view to establishing a settlement and creating a safe harbour for British ships that were constantly being attacked by pirates in the Indian Ocean. On the completion of the survey, General Charles Cornwallis, the East India Company's Governor of Bengal, immediately ordered the establishment of a penal colony on Chatham Island in the southeast bay of Great Andaman and named it Port Blair in honour of the captain. In 1792 the colony was moved to the northeast part of Great Andaman and named Port Cornwallis.[7] Because of disease and death, it was shut down in May 1796 and the native islanders were left alone for more than half a century.

Then came the Indian Mutiny in 1857, variously known as the Sepoy Mutiny, the Indian Rebellion and the First Indian War of Independence. The mutiny was largely a response to the company's harsh taxation and to its summary treatment of any opposition, though it began as an insurrection by Indian infrantrymen (sepoys) in the company's garrison in Meerut, near Delhi. Over the next year

[7] It is improbably suggested in some sources that Port Conrwallis was named not after Governor Charles Cornwallis but after his brother Admiral William Cornwallis, who had no involvement with the Andamans.

rebellions broke out elsewhere, both military and civilian—though the vast majority of Indians did not take part and most remained loyal to the Britain—and it took thirteen months for the company's army to quell the insurrection, with a key role played by Ghurka regiments. There were terrible atrocities committed on both sides. In 1858 Britain started to take over administrative responsibility from the company and offered an amnesty to all who were not accused of murder, but there was still huge pressure on Indian jails and this led to proposals to re-establish a penal settlement on the Andaman islands.

It was because of the mutiny that the islands were pressed into service a second time. A proposal for a new prison dates from April 1857 when a body called 'The Andaman Commission', headed by a Dr F.J. Mouat, was appointed to visit the islands and report on the best site for the settlement. The commission was advised by a Dr George Playfair on the medical and scientific needs of a settlement and a Lieutenant Heathcote who acted as hydrographer. As a result of the commission's work, a Captain Man was appointed to annex the islands and proceed with the establishment of the settlement under an experienced member of the Indian Jail Department, a Dr James Pattison Walker.

Walker, a member of the Bengal Medical Service, had already run another prison—in Agra—and had managed to keep control of it, using prisoners, during the 1857 mutiny. For this he was rewarded with the superintendency of the Andaman settlement. Here, he introduced the very strictest regime while being unable, as my grandfather writes, 'to maintain the same degree of discipline among convicts working in gangs in primeval jungle as can be insisted on within the four walls of a jail'. After three months in operation, the settlement had received 773 convicts from India. Of these, 64 had died in hospital, 140 had escaped and not been recaptured (assumed killed by the Jarawa), 87 had been hanged on conviction for escape and one had committed suicide, making a calamitous total of 292. Thus of the 773 convicts, only 481 remained in the settlement.

These were horrific figures and show that the repressive measures adopted by Walker, far from calming the atmosphere and discouraging attempts to escape, only aggravated the prisoners and made them more desperate. Walker was subsequently censured for unnecessarily harsh and repressive measures and resigned, or was moved, in 1859. In mitigation, my grandfather suggested, Walker was dealing with desperate men who had no hope of eventual release. In addition, his task was made all the more onerous because he had to rely on the notoriously lawless and undisciplined Naval Brigade for administration of the settlement and maintenance of discipline. The brigade's behaviour did not deter him, however. He immediately doubled their number and offered to house 10,000 convicts every year until they numbered 50,000. Fortunately his request was refused or ignored and he took up a new post as Professor of Hygiene at Calcutta Medical College.

Meanwhile attacks by the Andamanese were becoming more frequent and there were renewed requests for the British to deter the Andamanese from murdering shipwrecked sailors. Such requests were, as before, hampered by lack of knowledge of the islanders. According to Mouat, a Colonel Colebrook had visited the islands in the early 1800s and had published a 'short vocabulary of the language of the natives' but little more recent information had been acquired 'except through the narratives of shipwrecked persons, who invariably represented the aborigines as exceedingly savage and hostile.' A Dr Helps had tried to explore the islands in 1840, 'but he was murdered shortly after his arrival,' Mouat noted, adding 'The Andamaners were usually reputed cannibals', a claim now known not to be true.[8]

Interestingly RFL points out that the islanders seemed to realize that the convicts were under some sort of compulsion and aimed their attacks more on guards and warders than on prisoners.

A new spate of attacks started in early in 1859. They were chronicled by Maurice Vidal Portman (1860–1935), a British naval officer, born in Canada. In his book *A History of our Relations with the Andamanese*, he tells of an attack on 6 April 1859 which, though it was attributed to objections to the clearing of the forest, more fundamentally reflected the opposition of all twelve tribes to the presence of outsiders. (Some modern commentators assume that the tribes came together to eject the British but fail to appreciate that the tribes' basic mutual antipathy was to all outsiders, not to the British *per se*. Confusion arises also from commentators referring to the Ross Island Penal Colony, not appreciating that Ross Island

---

[8] 'Brief Narrative of an Expedition to the Andaman Island, in 1857', by F.J. Mouat M.D. of the Bengal Army, F.R.G.S. etc.

Andaman convict station on Ross Island in sight of the Governor's House (1872).

housed the islands' administrative capital. The convict settlement was always on the mainland at Port Blair, though there were what were called convict stations on Ross, Viper and Chatham islands. The islands never came under attack as none of the tribes had the means to mount a serious attack across water.)

One of the new series of attacks was on the Haddo encampment opposite Chatham Island when a number of prisoners were captured and induced by the Jarawa to dance with them. Then on 14 May came a major attack on the main convict station at Aberdeen which was overrun, occupied for several hours and looted. The attackers were dislodged by gunfire from the navy schooner *Charlotte* firing over the heads of the defenders, including men from the Naval Brigade, guards and some prisoners. Three days later came the main attack which was organized with some skill and came to be known as the Battle of Aberdeen. It might have succeeded had Walker not been warned of it. His informant was an escaped convict, Dudh Nath Tewari, who had been spared by the Jarawa a year earlier when others with whom he had escaped had been attacked and killed.

Uniquely, he had been allowed to live with the Jarawa, where he learnt to speak their language and married two of their women. He went on to discover their plans, and ran away on 23 April to report them. Thanks to his intervention the attack was repulsed. (Regarding these events, I find it strange that some historians now see Dudh Nath Tewari as a traitor and the failed Jarawa attack as the start of a freedom struggle. That suggests an ability by the Jarawa to conceptualise this idea of British colonialism and I do not think that is credible.)

Walker was succeeded briefly by a Captain Haughton (1859–62) and an R.L. Tytler (1862–64) who tried to improve the conditions at the camp, where the death rate of the prisoners was 700 per year and where, according to William Dalrymple, doctors at the camp reported that only 45 prisoners out of the 10,000 were considered medically fit.9 A Lieutenant Colonel Ford (1864–68) then followed and, under his command, a milder and more humane regime was introduced. Haughton held the position for more than two years during which time relations with the Andamanese took a turn for the better. They improved further when a Reverend Henry Corbyn, Chaplain of Port Blair, was appointed to head a new department to care for the Andamanese. He went on to found the hitherto-mentioned Andaman Homes, eventually opened in 1870, which had the objective of being points of contact with the Andamanese, a potential refuge for tribal people, and a focal point for the teaching of various crafts. As noted above, the Homes improved relations in the short term but had unfortunate longer-term results, because of their dependency on the Naval Brigade, and was soon seen as a mistake and abandoned. As my grandfather later wrote with perspicacity, 'the benefits of education were more than counter-balanced by the physical and moral deterioration resulting from the contact with civilization' yet he went on to observe that the Andamanese as a whole were 'quick and intelligent and learn readily *up to a point*. Beyond that the brain seems incapable of receiving impressions.'

Meanwhile relations with the Jarawa were broken off following the murder of more convicts, until it became clear that the attacks were not the responsibility of the whole tribe.

In 1868 Captain (later General) Horace Man, who had been appointed to annex the Andamans, assumed charge of the settlement and promptly introduced the same disciplinary system that had been developed for the penal settlements of the Malay

9 *The Last Mughal: The Fall of Delhi, 1857*, William Dalrymple, Bloomsbury, 2009.

Straights. By the time Man retired in 1871 the prison population had risen to a huge 8,373.

According to Nagendiram Rajendra in a paper of 1976, 'The system of discipline and management in force in the Straits could be termed the 'Association' system. Prisoners worked together during the day and at night slept together in open wards. There was no provision for religious instruction, and the accommodation provided was inferior. However, the prisoners enjoyed a greater amount of freedom, many being employed as messengers and orderlies without direct control of their actions and movements during the whole day. Moreover, the maintenance of discipline in prisons was mostly carried out by the prisoners themselves.'[10]

Although the India Office in London wanted to bring the Straits system more in line with the harsher solitary and silent systems that were in place in British jails, there was high-level support for the new approach from other quarters including the Viceroy of India, Lord Mayo, who visited the islands in 1872. Attracted by the prospect of an afternoon walk through the forest, he set off alone by boat from Ross Island towards Mount Harriet, which rises a thousand feet across the bay. On his return to his boat he was set on and killed by a convict hiding at the end of the jetty. The event was not allowed to disrupt the prison reform programme.

Meanwhile there had been two other significant developments: the establishment of a hospital for the Andamanese at Port Mouat as well as a school for aboriginal children on Ross Island. The latter was closed after a few years when, as RFL put it, 'it was found that the close contact with "civilization" was not in every sense beneficial.'

In 1874 the administration of the Andaman and Nicobar islands was switched from the Calcutta High Court to the Government of India. The next year came the appointment of Edward Horace Man, son of Captain Man, as head of the Andamanese Department. Man, with his long family attachment to the islands, took a special interest in the language, culture and lifestyle of the aboriginal tribes, even producing books of value to both future administrators and anthropologists. It is not clear from Grandfather's report whether it was known at that stage that there were twelve distinct tribal languages.

[10] *The Straits Settlements 1867–1874*, Nagendiram Rajendra, The Australian National University, Canberra, 1976.

In 1876 came the discovery that some of the friendly tribes of Middle and North Andaman had contracted syphilis and measles, as a result of contact with members of the Naval Brigade and through the trading links initiated and encouraged by the Andamans Commission with the aim of helping to fund the Andaman Homes. Trade was crucial for the Homes. Trading posts staffed by Indian *jemadars* (officials) had been set up along the coast to create commercial opportunities for the islanders in local products, and the money generated helped to fund Andaman Homes. As a result of these contacts, however, diseases spread rapidly, except among the unfriendly Jarawa of South Andaman and the Onge of Rutland and Little Andaman, with sufferers frequently being killed by fellow tribesmen in an attempt to stop them passing diseases to others. So little was the danger of transmission either understood or cared about that in 1878, convicts on release began to be allowed to settle on islands occupied by native Andamanese.

Thus was Grandfather prompted to write, over forty years later, that, 'generally speaking ... it would appear that the decline in the numbers of a tribe is in direct ratio to its contact with civilization.' He went on to conclude that one result of syphilis was that 'the small number of children, particularly of infants among the tribes, is I think due to resultant sterility being more or less universal.'

It was in 1870 that E.H. Man handed over charge of the Andaman Department to Portman. Portman's attitude to the tribespeople is unclear. On those rare occasions when pregnant tribeswomen took themselves to the new Port Mouat Hospital to give birth, Portman would send them back to their villages, saying that the jungles gave the babies a better chance of surviving. Was this heartless or caring? According to Ratan Chandra Kar a century later, there is a complete absence of infant mortality in the Jarawa today. The same could not have been said for hospital births a century and a half ago.

In all, the Andaman Homes experiment was a disaster, and the only tribespeople in whom there was no syphilis, measles or sterility were those Jarawa who had maintained their unbending opposition to all outside contacts. As RFL wrote, 'one result of these untoward circumstances was to impress on those responsible for tribal welfare that too close contact with civilization was altogether harmful to the race,' and attempts to induce the aboriginals to give up their nomadic life and settle down to regular occupations were abandoned.

Portman continued the ethnological and anthropological research started by Man. Both produced important studies that Ratcliffe-Brown recognized as the intellectual starting point for his own work between 1906 and 1908: Man's *On the Aboriginal Inhabitants of the Andaman Islands* (1885), which he was full of praise for and quoted extensively in his own book, especially when commenting on the administration's lack of success in inducing the tribes to work at anything more than what they regarded as the necessities of life; and Portman's *The History of Our Relations with the Andamanese* (1899) which he was less complimentary about and described as unreliable. Portman also prepared vocabularies of different Andamanese languages, befriending some of the aboriginals in order to pacify and get to know others, especially the Onge people of Little Andaman Island, but also using force against them on occasion.

After working in the Nicobar Islands, Man returned in 1899 and resumed responsibility for the Andaman tribes for another three years, eventually bequeathing his collection of Nicobar artefacts to the Pitt Rivers Museum in Oxford.[11] Meanwhile Sir Richard Temple, whose father and great-grandfather had been governors of Bombay, had taken over as commissioner and superintendent in 1894–95 and still occupied the post when my grandfather started his career with the India Office in 1901.

By now it had come to be appreciated that the misdemeanours of the Jarawa should not be attributed to the tribe as a whole but to individuals or cliques and that consequently there should be no mass punishment. During this time other lessons were being learned, including that close association with convicts and attempts to teach skills such as agriculture served no purpose, since the tribes seemed unable to acquire knowledge.

---

[11] The collection, fully catalogued by Man, included: canoe baler, coconut shell used for baling canoe partition for coconut loads, pig spear, toddy vessels and filters, cocoa nut ladle, scrapers for cocoa nut paste, hanging lamp, parrot stand, slow match, cycas paste strainer, cocoa nut leaf skirts, clothing of areca spathe and other material, fan for fanning fire, box of spathe, spathe bucket, box for holding fowls, feeding dish of areca spathe, betel box of spathe, box of pandanus leaves, cover of cooking pot, firesticks, bamboo joint containing lime, bamboo fire blowpipe, bamboo syphon and strainer, cane tongs, cane basket for garden produce, basket for carrying fowls, pig basket, basket sieve, cane strip for counting dogs, cane tally strips, coconut scraper of calamus, arca shell scraper, mytilus shell scraper, cyrena shell and cyproea shell used for pot making, ray fish grater, cloth of Celtis,

Attempts to start teaching tribal children were also abandoned. The only thing that did seem to interest the tribesmen was access to metal for the making of arrow tips. (I note that the incapacity of the islanders, who could be classed as palaeolithic hunter gatherers, to learn from outsiders stands in the greatest contrast to the enthusiasm for education of all the African tribes whom I encountered during my colonial service and subsequent business career in Africa.)

As the nineteenth century came to an end, the Jarawa occupying the country on the outskirts of the settlement resumed their periodic murder of convicts collecting forest products and of men employed by the Forestry Department, making it necessary that both should be accompanied by police guards. So great was the trouble caused that in 1902 the new commissioner sent out a small expedition of police and friendly islanders from North Andaman. Writing about the expedition in 1911 my grandfather says 'their object was to capture alive and bring into the settlement as many members of the hostile tribe as they could secure in order to have the opportunity to impress on them our power as well as our friendly intentions towards them'. The expedition failed and not a single Jarawa was captured. Moreover, in attempting a surprise night attack on a Jarawa encampment, the officer in charge of the Andamanese Department, a Percy Vaux, was fatally wounded by a tribal arrow.

A month before his death, Vaux wrote up an enlightening report about a successful tracking expedition that resulted in the capture of three young Jarawa. Assisted by two Andamanese trackers, Iragus and Henry, who explained that Jarawa camps were flanked by lookout huts, the team followed signs of Jarawa presence such as

---

bark cooking vessel, melodia fibre and other fibre, set of small cooking pots, objects used in pottery making, flat leaf cover used in cooking, grating put inside cooking pot, wooden scoop, pig trough, skewer, pig sticker, cocoa nut scoop, iron, hoe, rake, wooden scraper, broom, wooden pillow, cloth pillow, wooden colander, pole for fruit gathering, hooked pole for lifting traps, adze for canoe building, tools for scooping out canoes, loin cloth and skirt, object placed at grave head for containing objects used by deceased, v-shaped pegs for preventing the deceased from rising, hats used in burial feasts, leaf receptacle for catching wandering spirits, carved fish eagle charm, two charms on wood, fish traps, harpoon line basket, net trap, variety of cocoa nut, encrusted teeth of betel chewers, specimens of hair, bow and arrows.

snapped-off saplings but only came across the tracks of one man who appeared to be hunting and whose tracks led nowhere of significance. Then, in the early afternoon, the Andamanese helpers found a well-worn path that led up a hill and straight to a Jarawa camp.

'We approached it with the usual caution, only to find it empty,' wrote Vaux. 'It was a six-hut camp, arranged with the usual look-out huts at the sides; it had been left about a week, and there were only pig skulls and an old basket in it.'

Then, suddenly, the Andamanese noticed a column of smoke further away, and more huts. 'We approached and again found the huts empty. The occupants could only have left six hours before at the earliest. The logs were smouldering, boiled prawn heads were strewn about, water vessels made of leaves with water in them were in the huts, and everything betokened recent habitation. But no cooking pots or bones were in the huts, some baskets, arrows and a child's bow were all that we could find.'

Although the Andamanese doubted whether the Jarawa would return, Vaux waited in ambush for another hour and a half, then gave up and started the trek back to the shore, where they found a few Jarawa—two or three men, a woman and a child—who had evidently discovered the search parties' tracks and had pilfered two of their boats' four rowlocks. While the tribespeople had been tracking the trackers, however, other members of the penal colony launch had been tracking them in turn, but had come upon them too late in the day to hunt them further. Vaux commented that it was thoughtful of the Jarawa to leave two rowlocks to pull the boats back with, 'the only considerate thing I have ever heard of Jarawas doing'.

With the arrival of Radcliffe-Brown, a more scientific approach to the study of the Jarawa was adopted, and this led to a new difficulty: the difficulty in distinguishing between genuine artefacts and objects produced for commerce. As Kath Weston has written, 'once the residents of the Andaman Homes began to produce for retail fish arrows, baskets, models of Andamanese canoes, and copies of Chowra Island (Nicobari) pots' it started to be difficulty to separate anthropological finds and trophies made for the tourist market. By the early 20th century, she adds, all sorts of 'Andamanese curiosities' were available for sale, including wreaths of bones for one rupee, a 'skull ornament' for 50 rupees, and 'belts, as worn by Andamanese men and women' for two-to-four annas, 'obtainable either at the Andaman Homes warehouse or by ordering from one of the salesmen who made the rounds of the islands.'[12]

Meanwhile, as the era of convicts involved in the Indian Mutiny faded away, the Andamans evolved into what amounted to a new, prosperous and productive colony within the Indian Empire. Construction of the huge, modern Cellular Jail was completed in 1906 after ten years of construction. It was a stimulating and happy time for the Lowis family, with work challenges of all sorts for Reggie. I have written of the happy relationship, as recorded by my mother and my aunt Mary, that existed on Ross Island between the British and the trusted convicts. Elsewhere on the islands the convicts were involved in activities from manning the services on which the community depended to producing food including pioneering cash crops such as coffee, tea and rubber, starting new enterprises and building the infrastructure to support all the new development.

In this environment convicts and former convicts were evolving into pioneers. Pride and new feelings of ownership started to prevail. It was they, like the British convicts in Australia, who were their country's pioneers. Awareness that this was their role must have been a boost to their self-esteem and consequently to their skills and professionalism, and led to the rehabilitation of virtually every one of them.

By contrast, there are those in the twenty-first century who foster the idea that most of the convicts were political martyrs. Many of the mutineers of 1857–58 may have been but I saw no evidence of this in the Government of India reports of fifty years later. Figures for the numbers of convicts and their crimes show that among more than 11,000 convicts, most were murderers, with nearly 2,000 *dacoits* (bandits) and a smaller number of robbers, poisoners and rapists. There were also several hundred female prisoners, also mostly murderers, many of whom went on to marry fellow convicts.

My grandfather's report on the 1911 census gives credit to convicts in helping carrying out the count. He also details the

---

[12] 'Escape from the Andamans', Kath Weston, in *Central Sites, Peripheral Visions: Cultural and Institutional Crossings in the History of Anthroplogy*, ed. Richard Handler, *History of Anthropology* Vol. 11, University of Wisconsin Press, 2006.

amount of land under cultivation with the various crops including tea (166 acres), coffee (210 acres), vegetables, tamarind trees and even rubber, besides more than 2,000 acres of coconuts, which are not native to the islands. (Nor incidentally are bananas, which grow like weeds and have always been among the first crops planted by the new settlers.) The government report of 1922–23 gives figures for the employment of convicts. Working at the jail were 670, 394 were in forestry, 289 in cultivation, 254 in medical services, and most importantly 2,459 in running their own businesses. The fact that convict admissions to hospital in 1921–22 when he was still in overall charge of the commission were only thirteen compared with fifty the year before, with only a single death compared with five, is evidence for the effectiveness of his approach and a success story for which Reggie should take much of the credit. In addition, he justly acknowledged as early as 1911 that the involvement of convicts in the Andaman Homes experiment and in attempts to transfer skills to the aboriginals was a mistake.

I suppose it is both understandable and inevitable that since Indian independence, a different view of the convicts has taken root, and that they now feature as heroes and freedom fighters in a political narrative constructed by historians with an ideological antipathy to British rule. I accept that individual convicts may have played a part in the fight for India's independence but I think their importance in this respect is easily overstated, and cannot be considered a group phenomenon. As a group, what they can be remembered for is their pioneering work in building the Andamans into an economically successful enclave—part of India but also separate from it. It is this latter emphasis that I found predominant among the inhabitants of the modern Andamans even if the former is seen as giving the tourist industry, and academic literature, the bigger boost.

Chapter 10

My Family in the Andamans

My first family connection in the Andamans was George Anson, later Sir George, who was military superintendent in the 1880s and 90s. He came from a military family with several generations of service in India. For the last two years of the century he was joined on Ross Island at the entrance to the great harbour at Port Blair by his niece Bessie Coldstream who kept house for him and who then married Reginald Lowis.

The prospects for the young couple's start to married life must have been idyllic—unspoiled, pristine, tropical islands with beaches of coral sand and clear turquoise blue shallows inside dark fringing reefs. Beyond was the deep, dark-blue open sea stretching to more green islands, several just across the bay and others in the far distance. Though it was hot, the constant cooling of the sea breezes made it never unbearably so.

In the early days the Lowises lived with part of the British community in the great Port Blair Harbour, a few hundred yards from the shore, on Viper Island, named after the ship H.M.S. Viper in which Lieut. Archibald Blair arrived at the Andaman and Nicobar Islands in 1789.

From Viper, views across the bay would have revealed few signs of habitation apart from the roofs of the old prison and the military barracks peeping through the jungle. On the other side thick jungle rose to the summit of Mount Harriet at about a thousand feet. Other islands too, including Ross, had a forest cover with a scattering of houses and long views across the open sea to the outer islands.

My mother had the strongest memories of an early childhood of English nannies, friendly convicts and parents' dinner parties. What she remembered best were occasional visits to neighbouring islands where lived stark-naked native inhabitants of mysterious origin who, though they greeted her and her parents with loving embraces, had a reputation for greeting strangers with showers of deadly arrows.

On the highest point of Ross Island amongst the trees stood Government House where the Lowis family was destined to live for long periods in later years. Nearby was the Anglican church and the little hospital where my mother, her two sisters and their younger brother were born. Besides the other buildings were the barracks for the small garrison of British troops which complemented the Indian Army Garrison housed across the bay in Port Blair. In the bay in this penal colony of 13,000 lay the Indian Navy's RIMS *Dalhousie* on standby. Besides providing security she was on hand to transport members of the administration like my grandfather to the neighbouring Nicobar Islands, more than a hundred miles to the south and subject to the Andamans Commission (*see Appendix 5*).

By the time my grandparents began life in the islands, the convict settlement had existed for nearly fifty years. Port Blair was still very small, with a population besides the convicts of only some 4,000 civil servants, military and free settlers—that is, less than a third of the number of convicts. This made it about the size of a rural provincial capital in British colonial Africa.

The convicts were then, and had been for half a century, of vital importance to the development of the islands. As pointed out by the historian Prof. Clare Anderson, who knows the Andamans, those were the days of prisoner transportation, which included the movement of masses of people from Britain to Australia, where convicts built up the country. In the same era there had also been transportation between India and Mauritius. In places such as this, convicts were learning or developing all the skills needed to create a country that functions independently while also serving the British Empire. In later years my grandfather wrote of the reforming effects of jail and the transformation of convicts into useful citizens in this newly settled and fast-expanding part of the world.

My mother and my aunt Mary used to tell me how they were spoilt by doting convicts who fashioned leaves and sea shells into toys. There were female prisoners too, and they and male convicts with a record of good behaviour were allowed to marry. In the modern era it is the issue of these marriages who proudly see themselves as the descendants of pioneers, some honoured by election to the Local Born Society: a parallel, in many ways, to modern Australia.

My grandmother in her writings reveals a great warmth towards the convicts as she saw them. One example of feelings for their humanity and suffering comes out in an impassioned description she wrote of the lamentations of a prisoner under sentence of death and awaiting execution that she heard one night coming from his nearby place of incarceration. She looked forward also to the abolition of the death penalty many decades before it came about (*see Appendix 3*).

Bessie confirms in her writings that the main objective of government policy towards the convicts was their reform and rehabilitation, so that they would become useful citizens and so help provide for the self-sufficiency and economic development of the islands. In fact, by the time of Lowis's arrival, prisoners were only subjected to a regime of strict discipline in the Cellular Jail for the first months of their incarceration, or in the event of misbehaviour. After that the vast majority progressed to being useful, trusted collaborators in a joint enterprise including the development of the islands' potential to become a serious provider to India and the Empire of valuable timber as well as coffee, sisal and cotton.

Bessie's background and love of India were the reason why she had returned there after leaving school in England. Still in her teens, her organizing ability had been recognized when she was given charge of a tiger hunt and a jungle camping expedition for her father in the remote border regions near India's frontier with Nepal (*see Appendix 2*). Her competence and maturity were then rewarded when she was asked in the late 1890s to keep house for her uncle George.

Now, as they started their married life, Reggie and Bessie must have been excited by their prospects. They had much in common and had been brought to a beautiful friendly place with a house affording all-round views of an island paradise. I cannot help myself comparing what they had with how it was for new cadet or district officer arriving at an African bush station in the 1950s or early 60s. In Africa there might have been a small club and a tennis court and, if the community was lucky, a rough nine-hole golf course with 'greens' of oiled sand. Beyond the stimulus of a job almost entirely involving people and the wonders of the African bush, life on a bush station came with ever-present knowledge that six months of home leave was never more than three years away. For all but the exceptionally self-reliant, that was always a comfort.

Above: Watching cricket at the Ross Island Club. Below: Picnic—Bessie at centre.

Here on the Andamans, however, at the start of the twentieth century, the waiting time for home leave and long sea voyages could be nearly double that. A compensating factor was the club. It was a very superior affair. It was set in beautiful gardens with views over the harbour and included a ballroom where fancy-dress balls and plays were put on by the amateur dramatic society. There were lawn tennis courts and a well-maintained nine-hole golf course. Beyond all that the club could provide was the prospect of picnics beside empty beaches on miles of coral sand and swimming in crystal clear water protected by a fringing reef. On all the islands, the long beaches were hemmed in by a wall of enormous trees beyond which was nigh impenetrable jungle full of colourful birds and butterflies, as well as wild pigs and a unique species of fruit-eating cat.

Beyond the challenges of the job, all this might be considered as making for the ideal posting—but there was more. Besides regular sailing at the club, there was deep-sea and off-shore fishing for species such as tuna, bonito, barracuda and shark, and excellent seasonal shooting of snipe and oceanic teal visiting the islands.

It seems that my grandparents participated with enthusiasm in just about all that their new life had to offer. Reggie was a keen golfer, enjoyed shooting and fishing, and acted, playing the burglar 'Blackie' in the Amateur Dramatic Society's production of *Blackie's Little Brother*. Bessie played tennis. Mainly, though, she was occupied in writing and producing and caring for a family. After my mother Elizabeth's birth, Janet was born a year later and in successive years Mary and John. From the start there were British nannies who played a dominant role in the children's lives, freeing their parents for their busy social life. Mum's memories were of evenings when, elegant and shimmering in their finery, her parents would sally forth, leaving her and Janet with nanny.

A degree of antipathy started to build up however when, aged nine and eight, the girls were sent off to boarding school in England and did not see their parents for four years. As a result, the two came to resent their siblings, Mary and John, who seemed showered with affection from their parents that the older children had never enjoyed. It was they, not Elizabeth and Janet, who went with Bessie on her explorations of the sea shore with its the wonders of underwater gardens with coral and sea cucumbers and sea snakes, and small fish of every possible colour and combination of colours. It was they, too, who went on the family trips to meet islanders on North Andaman and, to a limited extent, following the 1911 census, on Rutland Island and Little Andaman.

Reggie found his new job varied and fulfilling, and was well suited to it. He soon gained promotion to assistant commissioner, his background in forestry working to his advantage as the government became more aware of logging and rubber as a potential source of income. He also put to use his ease in dealing with people. As time passed he travelled more widely around the islands and gained an unrivalled knowledge of them. He also used to pay regular visits to the trading posts and the Andaman Homes, as well as catering for and rehabilitating the convicts.

Bessie was a conventional home maker. Besides entertaining and family life, she wrote. She describes a voyage with Reggie over a

Reginald and Elizabeth: freed by their British nannies to enjoy a busy social life.

few days to visit the neighbouring Nicobar Islands which, though subject to the authority of the Andamans Commission, were utterly different from the Andamans with their population of islanders of oriental stock. Culturally and racially they were and remain utterly different from their historical northern neighbours the Andamanese. As noted earlier, they were open to outsiders and used to trading with other regions, including China.

While commissioners came and went, Reggie stayed and provided continuity, gaining more and more knowledge of the aboriginal tribes of whom so little was known. As a result, in 1911 he was appointed Superintendent of the Census in the Andaman and Nicobar Islands, part of an exercise taking place all over India, and managed to visit all the populated islands including the very special North Sentinel, 40 miles to the west of the main island chain. As far as possible he was able to include Bessie and the two younger children in these visits and there is the magnificent photograph (*see pages 88–85*) taken by a Captain Sir Henry Seton-Karr in 1911 of Mary, aged five, dressed in a flouncy lace dress and large hat confronting 20 or so naked Andamanese men and boys looking at her in some bewilderment. The photo is most likely to have been taken with Onge tribesmen on nearby Rutland Island.

Elizabeth and Janet Lowis: sent to boarding school and resentful of their sublings.

There was more contact after the census and there are pictures of Mary and John playing with and walking hand in hand with smaller Andamanese children (*see pages 47, 126 and 187*). Interestingly the aboriginal children who would normally have been stark naked have been provided with small strips of cloth to preserve their modesty. How the visits were set up and carried out I do not know but they seem to have been arranged with great care and sensitivity and there is every reason to imagine that they were seen as a public-relations triumph for Reggie and Bessie. The islanders also got good marks from Bessie when she dropped a valuable necklace in deep water off the coast and a boy was able to dive down and retrieve it.

The year after supervising the 1921 census Reggie retired, having served as acting commissioner, in sole charge, for long periods, particularly in his later years. His posting in the Andamans lasted longer than any ICS civil servant before or since. Before leaving office, he wrote a lament over the descent of the tribes towards extinction in which he argued, unusually, that the refusal of the Jarawa to cooperate with the authorities was suicidal, when it should have been apparent to all that it was only their self-isolation that had protected them.

Chapter 11

Discovering the Aboriginals

Following their discovery by the early navigators, worldwide awareness and understanding of the Andaman Islands and their aboriginal inhabitants was slow in coming. This was not surprising given their remoteness, the reputation of the tribes and the nature of the terrain. These fierce little people were seldom seen and could disappear in a twinkling with their bows and arrows into the thick forest where they became untraceable. There were few if any signs of their presence to be found and a visitor landing on an island beach could not expect a garlanded welcome.

In those early days visitors would have assumed if they caught a glimpse of these wild-looking people who inhabited all the main islands of the archipelago that they came from the same tribe rather than from twelve separate tribes all speaking different languages. Moreover most were mutually hostile, some more than others, because though they had canoes capable of crossing short stretches of water they could not cope with the longer distances between some of the islands. From the outset over the centuries and until very recently, nobody knew where these strange people came from or when. Even to well-travelled early visitors these were people like no others.

Not until the British in India started to take an interest in the islands in the late eighteenth century was there any knowledge of these aboriginal people beyond their hostility. Now it became apparent that they had no interest at all in any aspect of civilization or modernity, except metal for their arrow tips. They took no interest in cultivation and had never planted crops, not a single coconut, nor any tropical fruit.

The formal measure of British interest in the Andamans lies in the fact that it was thought worthy of a census, the first of which took place in 1871, with further censuses following every ten years.

Apart from what they said about new settlement, these headcounts revealed worrying changes in the number of indigenous tribespeople. Though there were estimated to have been about 3,500 Great Andamanese, for example, when the British established their penal settlement on the islands in the late 1850s, by 1901 there were only 625 left and just 209 in the sixth census in 1921, which Lowis said was an exact figure. (Since then their nine tribes—four in the north, five in the south—have become actually or functionally extinct.)

Lowis also reported in 1921 that numbers had dwindled so drastically that the Kols tribe had disappeared and there was only a single Bea. The population of the Onge, always fewer in numbers, was not found by any census to be in significant decline, dropping from 672 in 1901 to 631 in 1911, though it may have been much higher before. Most strangely, though, the census showed that the population of Rutland Island, which lies between South Andaman and Little Andaman, previously occupied by both Jarawa and Onge, had virtually disappeared, possibly because individual Jarawa had moved to South Andaman and individual Onge to Little Andaman to join the larger populations of their fellow tribesmen on those islands. Uncertainty about this indicates, however, the lack of ongoing contact between the government and tribes and the fact that over the ten years between 1911 and 1921 there had been no government visits to either island.

Up to 1911, and even to the next census in 1921, the physical presence of outsiders on the Andamans was barely apparent and a wilderness environment remained intact. It now seems odd that a group of fertile islands in the Bay of Bengal, relatively close to the Asian land mass with its own huge populations and close to much-used trade routes, should remain effectively untouched by the outside world until well into the twentieth century. It was not as if the islands were small. Several of them were larger than Mauritius in the Indian Ocean, on an equivalent latitude in the southern hemisphere. Mauritius has a similar climate and a population today of nearly two million, having been settled since it was discovered by the Portuguese in 1500s.

From the outset, the main preoccupation of the imperial British authorities was the penal colony and the convicts, not the locals. Relations with the twelve mutually hostile tribes were of no concern. Disunited, the tribes were more of an irritant than a threat, and with no missionary activity, no tribe seeking British protection against another, little investment in local resources, and no potential among them to provide manpower or skills to help exploit those resources, the usual incentives for colonization did not exist.

There is little to suggest that the tribes were ever well-enough coordinated or able to anticipate threats to come together to resist British occupation or to liaise in any other way. Most were separated by the sea, which their dugout canoes were incapable of crossing. The main centre of Port Blair had however been established at the southern tip of South Andaman, on land occupied by the Jarawa tribe, and was certainly a provocation. It was just to the north of Rutland Island and only a little further from Little Andaman, then both inhabited by the Onge and it was these two tribes that were to prove most actively hostile towards the new occupiers. Besides killing escaped convicts, in 1858 the Onge butchered a party of ten Chinese who had landed to search for water. The year after came the battle of Aberdeen, mounted by the Jarawa in a night attack on the penal settlement. Then in 1867 it was the Onge again who killed the crew of the *Assam Valley* on Little Andaman and attempted to kill their rescuers.

Modern historians and academics tend to adopt the view that Captain Archibald Blair's contempt for the tribespeople was typical of future administrators and that disregard was universal. I think this is an ideological view and I challenge it. Writing with obvious emotion and heartfelt conviction a century ago, Lowis said:

> It is clear ... that the decline [among some] of the Andamanese race can be attributed to the unfortunate effects of civilization, following our occupation of the islands. The policy of the government towards the Andamanese has been consistently humane and if at times it has been long-suffering, and if at times it has been short-sighted and disastrous in result, the fault is traceable not to neglect but to a laudable desire to improve the condition of the race. It was not realized until too late that to bring a people like the Andamanese too suddenly under the influence of civilization was altogether harmful.

Nowhere else has the issue been so well and so clearly expressed.

Even where attitudes to the islanders were unsympathetic, there was curiosity. Photographs of Andamanese islanders have been discovered in the Queen's Collection at Windsor Castle taken by the

French photographer Oscar Mallite in 1857 and 1858. Among these are some of an islander who was given the name of Jack, a young man who was captured and taken to Calcutta. There he met the Governor General, was photographed in military uniform and was treated as a curiosity before eventually being returned to the Andamans where, already ill, he succumbed to a disease to which he and his tribe had no immunity.

For there to be curiosity, however, there had to be at least some awareness. Of the Sentinelese on their small island to the west, there was very little. To an even greater extent than the Jarawa, they resisted all attention. In the days of the Raj, almost no effort was made to make contact except for the ten-yearly censuses and then, probably, only grudgingly. There was Commissioner Temple's visit in 1902, trying to track down the four escaped convicts, then nothing until my grandfather's abortive effort at a headcount in 1911. North Sentinel was not included in the 1921 census and no further visits were attempted for many years.

After Indian Independence the islanders became more assertive in demonstrating their wish to be left alone, by turning their backs on anthropologists and conveying defiance by means of obscene body language including assuming a defecating position. What this meant has never been properly translated but its message was clear.

The only known anthropologist not to have been deterred was Triloknath (T.N.) Pandit who always came bearing gifts. He alone succeeded in building a relationship, but was not always allowed to step ashore. His visits seem to have tailed off after the Indian government concluded that plying the islanders with gifts was inappropriate. Then came the time when an Indian Navy helicopter, checking on the islanders after the 2004 tsunami, was greeted by a volley of arrows. Most recently the Sentinelese message to the world has been reinforced by its killing of the American missionary John Chau. Meanwhile the Indian government continues to ban visitors from approaching closer than three miles. To this day there are still no firm figures on the size of the Sentinelese population. I find this somehow exciting and encouraging.

As a result of this separation, no research work has been carried out into tribal thought processes. No outsider has ever learned the Sentinelese language. Nor has there been any question of aboriginals on North Sentinel or anywhere else being subject to the law.

Up to 1922, when grandfather retired, in the rare event of a newborn baby looking as if he or she had been sired by an outsider, the child was killed. A recent case in Jarawa country shows that nearly a century later this state of affairs still applies. Anything and anyone that bridges the 60,000-year gap between our earliest ancestors and modern man is evidently not wanted. To this day most of the Indian settler community have never seen a tribesman and there are none to be seen in Port Blair.

From the start of his time in the islands right through his 22 years, Grandfather was in the forefront of senior administrators showing an interest in the tribes, travelling widely and promoting trade with the Great Andamanese in local products. This gave him the opportunity to gain new perspectives on the history and geography of the islands as well as on the social organization of the tribes and on their way of life. He stands alone in this respect. Radcliffe-Brown had carried out his research in the Andamans between 1906–08 and Grandfather's wide perspective, as revealed in his books, complemented what Radcliffe-Brown had done, but Radcliffe-Brown took twelve years to publish his work, which is probably why authority was slow to act on his findings and suggestions.

Reggie Lowis should probably have been mindful that even his own family's contacts had the potential to do harm to the islanders, if only because of the example they set. It is hard to see, however, how else goodwill and mutual understanding could have been

Reggie Lowis, photographed by Sir Henry W. Seton-Karr during the 1911 census.

established, other than by making at least minimal friendly contact. Such knowledge as existed in those days was limited and liable to be misinterpreted: the North Sentinelese were for example wrongly classified as Jarawa in Reggie's day. Only since the availability of DNA testing in the 1990s has our understanding been based any sort of solid scientific evidence.

Until T.N. Pandit's work with the Jarawa in the 1960s and 70s the tribes about whom most was known were the Great Andamanese and the Onge, thanks to Radcliffe Brown. He called them hunter-gatherers. Portman described how some Onge lived in mutually hostile communities called 'septs' until the food in the neighbourhood ran out or sanitary conditions made a move imperative. (Radcliffe-Brown wrote also that they inhabited areas where the British had granted them hunting rights but I have seen nothing to suggest that the British had the power to grant rights on Little Andaman or anywhere. They were not theirs to give. R.B. must have got this wrong.)

Though they might move from one location to another, groups would often return to places they had previously inhabited, and archaeologists have now found 'kitchen middens' (ancient waste dumps) of great historical interest because of the artefacts—bones, shells and pottery—that have been discarded over centuries.

Communities numbered between 20 and 50 people each and had a hunting area exclusive to itself. Somehow there was a natural balance between the size of the population and the land that sustained it. How this was so is yet to be understood.

Village accommodation was of three types: married, single male and single female. There was also an area reserved for dancing, an activity that assumed a high priority in village life and took place to celebrate joyous occasions such as weddings, successful hunts or even simply a good meal. (The style of dancing seems to me very similar to that of the Tonga of the Zambezi Valley, with much jumping up and down and a female chorus, but no drums.)

Grandfather wrote that the tribes came in two categories: those that lived mainly along the sea shore and had boats, and those that lived inland and had no familiarity with boats of any kind. The former were *Aryoto* and the latter *Eremlagers*. Boats were hollowed out tree trunks. The boat was the property of the man who had cut down the tree, even if others had helped him hollow it out.

There was a clear division of labour between the sexes. The men

Tribes were separated by the sea, which their dugout canoes were unable to cross.

were the hunters and fishers and made bows and arrows for hunting and warfare. Their implements were made from selected wood and, when available, their arrows were tipped with metal from shipwrecks, as previously noted. The tribes knew how to make rope and bows were strung with a strong and durable hibiscus fibre. Spears and harpoons were also made of metal, where possible, and used to hunt turtles and dugong. In recent times some hunting has been carried out with dogs first introduced by Burmese forest workers.

Women would collect food, digging up roots with a special digging stick and gathering a variety of nuts, leaves, seasonal fruits and honey which besides being an important part of their diet had a number of medicinal properties. They also caught prawns, crabs and small fish, collected firewood, and cooked. Quoting E.H. Man, Reggie wrote: 'In their natural state the Andamanese have no occupations beyond those connected with the procuring and preparation of food.' Besides enjoying a healthy lifestyle and a balanced diet, they had access to clean water and levels of personal hygiene were high.

Not having the ability to make fire, according to Radcliffe-Brown, made the Andamanese unique in the world, and the tribes would nurture live coals in their villages which they took with them on their travels. (A century later Dr Ratan Chandra Kar has said that the Jarawa can make fire but not whether this skill has been newly acquired.)

Given the reputation of the tribes for killing all visitors, their customs of warfare among themselves seem highly delicate. There was no such thing as a stand-up fight, the art of fighting being to take your enemy by surprise. Having done so, an attacker would kill one or two of the enemy and then retreat. If the attackers came across strong resistance or lost a man, they would retire. There is no evidence of full-scale war ever having taken place among the tribes.

Great importance was attached to skills associated with hunting and warfare as well as such qualities as generosity, kindness and freedom from bad temper. People with these qualities gained respect and influence, and their opinions carried the most weight. Though there was no local word for 'chief', Radcliffe-Brown says

The men fished with spears and bows but women also caught prawns and crabs.

that early officers of the Andaman Homes chose tribal intermediaries to whom they gave the Indian title of '*raja*'.

There was no formal governing body but a universal respect for
age and seniority. This meant that society was regulated entirely by
older men and women. The young were brought up to respect and
defer to their elders, for whom there were special terms of address.
One example of good manners was that the best part of a pig hunted
by a younger man would go to the elders.

Despite the lack of formal leadership, some individuals were
credited with having supernatural powers that gave them authority
over their fellows. Among the Great Andamanese they were '*Aka-Jeru
oko jumu*' meaning literally 'the one who speaks from dreams'. Such
individuals had a particular influence over society. Respect is
conveyed by the term '*da*' for a woman. As in much of Africa the
most respectful term of all for a woman is '*Mama*', a word used by
the Andamanese tribes that has gone round the world and may have
originated in Africa.

There were no formal sanctions for anti-social behaviour or
punishments for crime. It was up to the individual who had been
wronged, or was the victim, to seek retribution. At the same time an
individual's antisocial behaviour resulted in loss of social esteem
and that was seen as punishment enough. Serious quarrels were
kept to a minimum by the influence of older men. Children who
misbehaved were reprimanded but never punished. Radcliffe-Brown
said that demonstrations of anger were brought to an end by a show
of authority. He added that he had never heard of a case of murder.
Theft was very rare.

Most significantly in this highly interdependent society, laziness
was regarded as anti-social. Every man was expected to take his
proper share in providing food for himself and others. No
reprimand would be made to a shirker but he would find himself
demoted to a lesser rank, given smaller and less desirable cuts of
meat and left out of discussions on important issues.

Another class of wrong was the contravention of ritual
prohibitions such as the killing of a cicada. Such contraventions
could only be punished by supernatural interventions controlled by
ancestors. (I saw similar traditions in parts of rural Africa, but here,
African witch doctors exercised more power and influence than
Andaman medicine men.)

Family life was of the greatest importance and arose from

marriage. Society being monogamous, it was the duty of husband and wife to avoid sex outside marriage. At the same time, promiscuous intercourse before marriage was perfectly normal. Marriage was only normally permissible between couples who were not even distantly related; marriage between first cousins was forbidden. Unattached men would go visiting, preferably to the most remote villages, in search of a wife. (I have seen a similar practice among the Tonga people of Zambia, called 'ku *swaya swaya*' or 'ku *pota pota*'. It is an effective way of avoiding conditions caused by recessive genes.)

All the tribes were monogamous, with the men preferring to take their wives from villages as distant from their own as possible, while still within their tribal area. Marriage was taken seriously but not regarded as fully consummated until the birth of a child. Typically males would marry in their late teens, females two or three years earlier. Marriage customs would include the couple adopting a demeanour of bashfulness towards each other. The groom would also sit on his bride's lap while gripping her tightly by the wrist, and the grip had to be maintained. Reggie describes an incident he witnessed when the groom was asked to help launch a boat to transport the newly-weds. Having released his grip, the bride sped off into the forest and escaped.

In the case of a more pliant bride, the couple would link arms around each other's necks. Following the nuptial ceremony they would then retire shyly to a hut that had been prepared for them while friends continued dancing. In the early days it was regarded as comely for them to continue to behave as if shy of each other. Meanwhile they were abundantly supplied with food by others.

Children were not weaned until they were three or four years old (though Dr Kar says two), were regarded as belonging to the community as a whole and were spoilt by everyone in the village. Fathers would make toy bows and arrows for their sons, and sometimes a toy canoe or spear, and teach them to make these themselves. Girls would accompany their mothers gathering food. Children and were frequently adopted by other parents after the age of eight but would retain a strong relationship with their birth family through frequent visits. They would be known by a birth name or nickname. For girls this changed when they reached puberty, when they received a new name, perhaps of a tree or a plant in flower at the time. Thereafter only that name was used.

There were strong conventions in tribal society governing the behaviour of men and women towards each other. A married man would not have close dealings with the wife of a younger man. It was not considered fitting that he should even speak to her, and if communication was absolutely necessary it had to be through a third party. He could certainly not touch her. On the other hand no such strictures were placed on relationships with the wives of men older than himself. Widows and widowers would remarry after a spouse's death.

Strict conventions also applied to the relationship between a married couple and their respective in-laws, known as 'aka-yat'. These were reflected in strong inhibitions amounting to a sort of shyness, which meant that they had almost nothing to do with each other except send each other presents.

Tribespeople liked to give and receive presents and it was considered impolite to refuse to give over anything for which one was asked. Under normal circumstances what was requested was handed over immediately, so that possessions seemed to be almost continually changing hands. By convention, a younger man would never make a gift request of an older.

Hosting was highly regarded. Visitors usually stayed for a few days and were entertained with hunting, feasting and dancing, with new songs composed for the occasion, and the giving of presents. Disputes could arise, however, when visitors felt the level of hospitality they had received had not been sufficiently high.

The climate in the Bay of Bengal is warm and nudity has always been normal. Experience shows that it is healthier than wearing even limited clothing, which left unwashed is unhygienic and can harbour infections or disease. Over the years, when well-meaning outsiders gave clothes and blankets to tribespeople, health problems invariably followed.

For men and boys, dress was always limited to a necklace and a belt, though in recent times some have started wearing loin cloths in the company of outsiders, a sign that inadvertent evolution can take place. The Jarawa and other tribes would also use a fine, white clay to decorate the body, as well as a red paint derived from turtles. Red was the colour most favoured by the tribes.

Women would wear a belt from which they suspended a bunch of leaves in the front. They also wore bones, human or animal, suspended from necklaces. Widows were likely to wear their deceased husband's jaw bone, or even his skull. Besides providing decoration, the bones were supposed to prevent or cure illness.

The role of spirits known as 'lau' in North and Middle Andaman was of great importance in tribal society. When a person died he or she became a jungle or sea-spirit lau or, in South Andaman, a sky spirit. All spirits were thought to exercise an influence over the living in much the same way as in some parts of rural Africa to this day. The spirits were believed to be the cause of all sickness and death from sickness. As a individual wandered in the jungle or by the sea shore the spirits were liable to come upon him invisibly and strike him, whereupon he would fall ill and might die. Radcliffe-Brown concluded that

> the Andaman islanders as a whole personify the phenomena of nature with which they are acquainted, such as the sun and the moon. In modern times the closeness of their relationship with nature and natural phenomena has been shown to be at a level which modern man lost a very long time ago.

This is a factor of potentially incalculable value to modern man and one of the many reasons why the preservation of unadulterated Andaman culture must be one of our top priorities as we come to appreciate the need to restore a relationship with nature that is fundamental to our survival as a species.

The family visits of Bessie and Reggie to the tribespeople could not have involved conversation because of the language problem but involved plenty of body language including touching, all building trust and understanding. They were a unique departure from the norm and accorded with Reggie's determination to move away from stereotypes and put relations on a new warm basis, recognizing a mutual humanity. They amounted to a great triumph for Reggie.

It was my cousin Iain, Uncle John's son, who lent me the photograph of an Onge man and woman arriving at Ross by canoe from nearby Rutland Island (*see page 76*). On the back of the photo someone has added a note, explaining that the tribespeople had brought a gift of dugong tusks for our grandparents. Clearly these supposedly savage, stone-age aboriginals had been touched by the kindness they had received.

A turning point in Reggie's career came with his appointment in 1911 as superintendent for the Andaman and Nicobar Islands element in the India-wide census of that year. His report, later published as a book, sheds light on the whole gambit of the geography and history of the islands but is remarkable for its emphasis on the tribes.

In it he stresses that the importance of the census lay not in counting prisoners, members of the military and police, or even the growing numbers of settlers but in recording numbers and movements of the different tribes. His great interest in them never ceased to grow and he acknowledged the cooperation on tribal issues he had received from Radcliffe-Brown and E.H. Man.

It was also Reggie who started to realize that efforts to civilize and to make contact were both counter-productive and dangerous, however well intentioned, leading to illness and sedentary torpor. 'For many years,' Reggie wrote, 'attempts were made to teach the

Andamanese cultivation and different hand crafts but without success. They would work at them only so long as they were forced to do so and then left to themselves they always lapsed into their original condition.' He added, 'The Andamanese will not on their own accord perform the simplest agricultural operations. The race as a whole has shown today the same disinclination to take to regular employment as they displayed when they first began to come under our influence 50 years ago.'

It was thanks to Reggie that a belated understanding started to arise that the Jarawa and Sentinelese wished to be left alone, even though he wrote that their refusal to bow to government authority might end in their undoing, and he brought to an end attempts to train and educate them and what was called 'mainstreaming'. It also started to be realized that it was only the friendly tribes that were

'Family visits from the tribespeople involved lots of body language and touching.'

being wiped out. There had been no outbreaks of disease amongst the Jarawa, the Sentinelese or the Onge. The conclusion was clear. The blame all lay with unwanted contact, outsiders including convicts, the naval brigade, settlers and people involved with the trade in local products and with Andaman Homes.

As an administrator, Reggie felt he sometimes had occasion to apply sanctions in response to unacceptable behaviour by the tribes, but he also accepted that these were almost always futile. One of his books includes a copy of an account by a Mr Fawcett of a punitive expedition that he led on the Jarawa in 1910. Like the 1902 expedition, it was a total failure. In a night raid, all that was achieved was the capture of a single woman. The Jarawa all escaped into the night, their flight spurred on by volleys of blank cartridges. The concluding extract from the report speaks volumes:

> Failure of the expedition to achieve more decisive results after surrounding the Jarawa on 20 March is principally due to a laudable though possibly mistaken desire to avoid bloodshed. Orders were given to commence firing with blank ammunition in the hopes that the Jarawa terrified by the firing and realizing the hopelessness of resistance to such odds would surrender at distraction! That this presumption was wrong proved by results. It is hoped however that the Jarawa will have learnt a lesson and that it will have a salutary effect on them as the one of 1902.

The breadth of Reggie's new understanding and conclusions had a considerable impact. There came a new official understanding that the attitude of the unfriendly tribes towards civilization was entirely logical. For the tribes, to stay alive meant to stay away, and so all attempts by the administration to train and educate them and introduce so called 'mainstreaming' ceased. All this reflected very well on Reggie. What was not clear was what the right policy should be in terms of those islanders who had already lost their autonomy and how other aspects of the islands' development should be handled.

During the years leading up to Reggie's retirement the numbers of 'friendly' Great Andamanese continued to fall, so that by the time of the 1921 census, which again he supervised, the five southern tribes of North and Middle Andaman were either extinct or about to go extinct—the Kols had disappeared, and there was only a single Bea—while the four northern tribes had just handfuls of individuals. By contrast, the 'unfriendly' Jarawa were holding onto their numbers by keeping themselves isolated. The main difficulty lay with the people who fell between these extremes. At one point during the census visit to Little Andaman, Reggie's census party spotted a family of Onge on the shore near Jackson Creek. They landed and during a friendly exchange handed over presents.

The increasing willingness of the Onge to engage led, after Reggie's retirement, to more settlement being allowed on their territories than Reggie thought wise. Even traditional Jarawa territory on South Andaman saw a relaxation by the authorities of the disposal of land for settlement to released convicts and others, to ex-servicemen after Indian independence and subsequently to refugees from Burma and the former East Pakistan, now Bangladesh.

With his promotion to deputy, Reggie spent more and more time acting as commissioner, to the point that the family spent more time in residence in Government House on Ross Island than at home. Almost his last act was the 1921 census in which he discovered an unexplained remnant of five Jarawa on Havelock Island but once again failed to count the Jarawa on South Andaman and did not even try to visit North Sentinel, for fear of attack. In his 1921 report, Reggie includes an account by a Mr Field of a 1920 Jarawa raid on a party of 22 convicts. He does not give the number killed but says the attackers stole mainly metal for arrow tips. Because the raiders wore red and white loincloths, the convicts said they were not Jarawa. It is hard to imagine, however, what other tribe they might have been.

In my view, Reggie was a man before his time. Half a century before the discovery of DNA he seems to have stumbled on the truth when writing about the tribes: 'They remain a remnant of a forgotten race, living the same life and using the same basic weapons as did their ancestors many thousands of years ago.' The thought preyed on him.

By the time Reginal Lowis retired from the Indian Civil Service in 1922 and he and Bessie went off to try life in Canada, the British had ruled for 130 years. Thanks to such administrators as Captain Man, his son E.H. Man, Reverend Henry Corbyn and Sir Richard Temple, a system had been set in motion for the development of the islands. By the standards of their time, those regimes appeared to be largely enlightened; looking back, we can see they took place at the cost, albeit unintended, of the virtual extinction of nine of the Great Andamanese tribes.

My grandfather stands out as seeing that loss as an unacceptable trade-off. In this respect his insight was substantial; it was tragic that he came on the scene too late to reverse much of the damage that had already been done. It is tragic, also, that the research and professionalism of the anthropologist and academic Radcliffe-Brown, and the depth and detail of his work in describing tribal life and culture and the preoccupations of tribal people, had not taken place earlier and was not published sooner.

There were always three major policy issues for administrators of the Andaman islands. The economic expansion and well-being of settlers was one; the fate of the aboriginals was another; the third was the hosting of the penal colony. As foreseen by my grandfather from the early 1920s, the colony would have to be run down. What he did not predict was the re-emergence of Indian nationalism. As opposition to British rule started to build in the 1920s, the Cellular Jail began to fill with growing numbers of people whom the Indian nationalists would term political prisoners, but whom the authorities had charged for breaches of the peace, assaults, killings and other more specific crimes. Given the rising tide of unrest, it was regarded as a better option for such people to be sent to the remote Andamans than to be a destabilizing influence on family, friends and fellow prisoners while festering in detention in jails on the Indian mainland.

Unsurprisingly, the Cellular Jail regained the divisive reputation that the older penal settlement had acquired in the years after the 1857 Sepoy Mutiny. Unsurprisingly also, it divided and exacerbated the memories of people who lived through Independence and for generation afterwards. Writing on social media in 2017 Anup Dasgupta, born 1944, mentioned the 'sinister punishments' that he says his father Sushil Dasgupta experienced as part of the prison's regular routine: 'slave work, torture, a starvation diet and brutal forcefeeding'. It seems Sushil Dasgupta was an activist who had been involved in a robbery at gunpoint to 'raise funds' for the Jugantar party, and then got into a shoot-out with police. He was then arrested, convicted and sentenced to transportation to the Andamans. That was in 1932. The sad story does not end there, as after his release in 1943, Sushil was fatally stabbed during communal riots in his hometown of Calcutta.

It is evident that the regime at the Cellular Jail was not an easy one, but it is important to stress that there were other factors in this case beyond the purely political. From 1932 to 1937, prisoners took part in a series of hunger strikes, one of which, starting on 12 May 1933, went on for 45 days. These eventually prompted Mahatma Ghandi to make representations to the head of the British administration in India, Lord Linlithgow, with the result that the jail was finally closed and the prisoners repatriated to India. In complaining about the starvation diet, Sushil may have been referring to the strike.[13] This is not, however, to exonerate the prison authorities from running what may very well have been a harsh facility.

In October 1942, following the December 1941 attack on Pearl Harbour and the occupation of Singapore in February 1942, the Japanese took over the Andaman Islands. The islands were already in a weakened state, after suffering a colossal earthquake of magnitude 7.7 to 8.1 in June 1941 which killed as many as 8,000 people, devastated many of the buildings and caused the British to abandon their settlement on Ross Island. (It is now a ruin and a memorial, as described earlier, with the roots of great trees growing

[13] https://www.independent.co.uk/news/long_reads/cellular-jail-india-integral-country-fight-freedom-independence-british-colony-andaman-and-nicobar-a7883691.html

through and over the walls of Government House, the church and other buildings.)

The Japanese seem to have found the social dynamics of the Andamans incomprehensible, not understanding Britain's imperial and colonial role or its ambiguous relationship with people on the ground. They seem to have been especially puzzled by the fact that the settlers did not see the British as oppressors and that many harboured some loyalty towards the British and did not welcome their Japanese 'liberators' with open arms. Such feeling fueled suspicions, however, and resulted in many, mainly prominent people, being shot by the Japanese on suspicion of spying. In all, 2,000 people died and 500 were tortured during the Japanese occupation. At the same time, as described above, the Japanese became obsessed with the idea that British spies were being harboured by the tribes, and carried out bombing raids on the unfortunate Andamanese, particularly the Jarawa.

Meanwhile the Japanese took the opportunity to introduce and encourage the first presence of the the Indian National Army (the INA) on Indian soil. However they seem to have been regarded more as collaborators than liberators by the settler population. Netaji Subhas Chandra Bose, the INA founder, joined them for a short time but while he enjoyed the enthusiastic support of the Japanese, he seems to have gained little or none from the locals during his short stay. He was of course kept away from anyone whom the Japanese might suspect would tell him what was really going on.

The fact was that there was indeed a significant British presence, all of it on Middle and South Andaman, from the start of the occupation in 1942 to the Japanese surrender in 1945, but it was never detected, nor was there ever any contact between these British and Indian soldiers and the tribes.

Small parties of Special Operations Executive (SOE) soldiers had been landed undetected on the coast by submarine with large quantities of arms, radio equipment and other stores which were carefully hidden. The first party, led by Dennis McCarthy, who had been superintendent of police in the Andamans before the war, was required to obtain details of Japanese strong points and other information of potential use in retaking the islands. It travelled as far south as a Ferrargunj on South Andaman, only a short distance north of Port Blair. McCarthy and his party made contact with the local settler headman who invited the soldiers into his house and briefed them on the horrors of the Japanese occupation, including the murder of a Mr Bird, the secretary of the chief commissioner, and subsequent killings, assaults and rapes. The conversation with the headman was interrupted by the chance arrival of Japanese soldiers and a local interpreter. The headman invited the SOE men into the central room of the house so that McCarthy and a soldier called Habib Shah could hear what was discussed. On the departure of the Japanese, the party was able to slip out of the house and return to the jungle. Unfortunately, on the return journey to base, Habib Shah spotted a way through some dense jungle, slipped on his sten gun which went off, and was killed almost instantly.

That first landing, named operation Baldhead 1, was followed by others, all carried out in secret. When British and Indian troops eventually landed at Port Blair in September 1945, the Japanese not only offered no resistance but proved surprisingly cooperative. Their attitude apparently had something to do with the fact that they still had not known of the SOE's presence right through the war.[14]

During the period between the world wars and before Indian independence little changed to affect the tribes. With the Great Andamanese virtually extinct, the remaining Jarawa on Rutland Island moved to South Andaman and the Onges consolidated themselves on Little Andaman. Now classed as friendly, they became more dependent on government handouts and their numbers dropped. The number of Jarawa on South Andaman remained stable.

Indian independence in 1947 brought no major move from the broad British policy of leaving the tribes alone. It did however bring in new settlers from all over India, many of whom went to live in areas formerly regarded as tribal land. Most were ex-service people who joined their ex-convict compatriots in building the new Andamans. There were also refugees from Bangladesh and Burma. But what was to become of the Jarawa?

---

[14] See *Special Operations in South-East Asia 1942-1945: Minerva, Baldhead and Longshanks/Creek* by David Miller, Pen & Sword Military, 2015.

Chapter 14

African Perspectives

In his report on the 1911 Census of the islands, Reggie comments on the reasons why there had apparently been no historic problem of over-population among the twelve tribes in the Andamanese islands. There was no polyandry, child murder or the procuring of abortions that might have controlled the birthrate, he says. The key factor in population control had therefore to be the death rate, and this by implication was what must have kept the islanders in a natural balance with their environment for thousands of years.

More recently Dr Ratan Chandra Kar has said that he encountered no cases of menstruation problems among Jarawa women, no abortions or multiple births, even of twins, no death in childbirth, no congenital malformation, no problems with lactation and only one case of an infertile couple. Family planning was neither wanted nor needed. The health and numbers of the tribes seemed somehow to be self-regulating. There was also no record of tetanus, cardiac dysfunction, psychiatric and thyroid disorder, varicose veins and obesity. Tooth decay was rare and there have so far been no cases of HIV or AIDS amongst the Jarawa. Besides diet, lifestyle and the environment, Dr Kar attributes the general good health of the aborigines to their lack of contact with the modern world.

My own perspective on the Andamanese was shaped by my experience growing up in what was then India, now Pakistan, and by my work in Africa. I have said that I have always been struck by the shocking fact that even up to my grandfather's time as acting commissioner, not a single outsider was able to speak any of the Andamanese languages. The situation was the very opposite of that which prevailed in the Indian Civil Service in mainland India and in the Colonial Service as I encountered it in Africa, where communication in general, and the learning of local languages in particular, was a top priority.

Dr Kar is I think the first outsider to have become genuinely fluent in an Andamanese language. Until he started working with the Jarawa in the late 1990s, our failure to communicate properly in the Andamans could only have exacerbated deep native antipathy towards outside influences, including British, and the desire to be left alone. Our resistance to them was met by their resistance to us. It must also have been a factor in their resistance to change, a factor I did not encounter in all the years I spent in Africa, except perhaps amongst the Bushmen of the Kalahari. My experience of African cultures leads me to believe that Africans in general have embraced change more readily than other cultures I have encountered.

A contributory factor in the failure of the British administration to learn any of the tribal languages was the lack of commitment to the Andamans by those posted to run it. Senior civil servants and military came and went with too much frequency to build very much local expertise. Over nearly two centuries of British rule only a handful of officials stayed for more than five years. Grandfather Reginald outserved them all, lasting for 22 years.

As a consequence, little was ever understood about the needs of the tribespeople and how best to protect their interests on a spectrum between intervention and disengagement. Absolutely fundamental, however, is the question of understanding who these people are, what they represent and what the loss of them would entail for the world, not just in terms of statistics or anthropological theory but in terms of our understanding ourselves and our needs as fragile creatures of nature rather than as the sophisticated product of modern deracinated processes.

Grandfather, writing in 1911, said that the Jarawa looked as if their origins were African and for me, following a career entirely involving Africa, they were clearly African, but there seems to have been no further work on this, in spite of the cultural studies of E.H. Man, Portman and Radcliffe-Brown until the arrival of Professor Hagelberg, mentioned earlier. This protagonist and heroine came across a cluster of human hair in a dusty glass cabinet in Cambridge, carried out DNA testing and discovered a link with Africa, specifically with pygmies from the Southern part of the continent, going back 60,000 years.

For Hagelberg, the implications of the DNA results were enormous and she could hardly wait to visit the Andamans, and specifically Little Andaman, to collect more. She arranged to travel to the islands with Dr Lalji Singh, the Director of India's Centre for Cellular and Molecular Biology. The 1991 visit, perhaps arranged too hastily, turned into an agonizingly frustrating failure, with layers of officialdom blocking her way. While she waited for the authorities to make up their mind, Hagelberg fell back on taking DNA from domesticated local pigs to compare with the wild variety living in the forest. She never did get to visit Little Andaman on that trip. She and Lalji had run into a brick wall.

Hagelberg returned to Norway and planned a second visit with Lalji in 2001. This time she managed to get specific authorization from the government in New Delhi. Even then, the scientists found all sorts of blockages placed in their way. There were arguments about their being accompanied by a British film crew, whether out of a genuine sensitivity to the islanders or because the local authorities had something to hide or did not want their tribal policy opened up to journalistic scrutiny. Then, after the obstructions seemed to have been cleared, a lone policeman patrolling on Little Andaman blocked Hagelberg's way, leaving Singh to continue alone. It was only by chance that on her return to Port Blair, her party came across a boat carrying some Onge tribesmen and she was able to get some samples of hair from them.

Singh meanwhile gained permission to take DNA from 46 Onge tribesmen and blood samples from a handful of Jarawa. He found that the Y chromosome of the Jarawa blood was missing an ancient genetic mutation characteristic of African races which was present in the Onge DNA. This suggested that the Jarawa had migrated before the Onge and that they came from elsewhere. These investigations led to some surprising conclusions. It transpired that whereas the Onge had arrived on Little Andaman some 40,000–60,000 years ago, the Jarawa must have arrived some 50,000 years earlier and were not related to any of the Andamans' other aboriginal groups. The two tribes must then have evolved in isolation not just from the outside world but from each other. This would help to explain the mutually unintelligibility of their speech.

New Delhi has since allowed Singh to collect more samples from the Jarawa for scientific analysis, in the hope that that their DNA might hold the key to the eradication of diseases such as malaria.

As for the Sentinelese, whom no one has yet studied, Singh considers them the only pre-Neolithic tribe left in the world. He adds, 'These people have been able to survive by natural selection without any interference from modern medicine for thousands of years. Their genes are living proof of the survival of the fittest,' a strange reversal of Wetsern civilisation's assumptions about progress and evolutionary success.

How these African people reached the Andamans is a question that can only be guessed at. The DNA suggests that they travelled in separate tribal groups and arrived over a long period of time—centuries or even millennia. The distance from southern Africa to the Andamans is 8,000 km (5,000 miles). I imagine these brave people, the first human beings, the men with their bows and arrows, the women carrying babies and small children, setting off into the great unpopulated unknown. They will have made their way down river valleys, probably the Limpopo or the Zambezi, stopping for years, decades or even centuries where local fruits and animals to hunt were plentiful. No one can know what spurred them and what their route was across the vastness of what had yet to become the Indian Ocean. Eventually, in what is now the Bay of Bengal, volcanic activity and the invasion of the sea left them marooned on islands where for tens of thousands of years they lived untouched and unchanged by the outside world.

The theory that their African appearance derives from a life in an environment similar to Africa's but not African now seems implausible.

The Andaman DNA discoveries have since led to further researches drawing attention to wider connections with the world. In a study in 2017, Dr V.K. Kashyap of Hyderabad's Central Forensic Science Laboratory, and others, have shown that the Andaman aboriginals are part of an early human dispersal across South-East Asia. While pointing out that some of the Great Andamanese tribes as well as the Jarawa represent independent DNA clusters, the Andamanese as a whole must either be surviving descendants of African migrants, or founder populations of modern humanity, or possibly both.

In another study, Partha Majumder, founder of the National Institute of Biomedical Genomics in Kalyani, West Bengal, suggests that the DNA of the Onge and Jarawa tribespeople gives evidence of a hitherto unrecognized humanoid. Writing about this in the English-language edition of the Israeli newspaper *Haaretz* in 2016, Ruth Schuster, who covers archaeology and science news, quotes

Majumder as saying that 'this mysterious hominin coexisted with the Neanderthals and Denosivans, but was a different species. No remains of it have been found yet—just distant echoes of its genes in Andaman islanders existing today:

> The research produces a new branch on the tree of human evolution, starting with an Unknown Ancestor some 600,000 years ago. Homo sapiens and Neanderthals split off from that Ancestor, and Denisovans later split off from the Neanderthal branch.
>
> It now seems that a third species, the newly discovered one, also split off from that Unknown Ancestor.
>
> Later in the course of history, Homo sapiens who left Africa mated with Neanderthals. Members of that human-Neanderthal mix continued on to Asia, where they split into a host of peoples. And at least some of those people, the ancestors of the Andaman islanders checked in this study, mated with the third ancestral species.
>
> Flash forward to now: the only population not to contain any Neanderthal or Denisovan genes (insofar as has been tested so far) are Africans. In other words, the interspecies sex with both happened after the split between the early Homo sapiens who left Africa and those who remained.[15]

Very interesting. And on 28 October 2019—the very day I completed the first draft of this book—came news in the journal Nature of research on the origins of mankind carried out by Professor Vanessa Hayes, referred to earlier, of the Garvan Institute of Sydney, Australia. What fascinates me is that it bears out Erika Hagelberg's conclusion on the southern-African origin of the DNA of the Cambridge hair sample.

But Hayes's findings are more specific than that. They show that the earliest human beings came from the vast wetlands of what is now Botswana, which 200,000 years ago formed an oasis covering thousands of square miles surrounded by impenetrable desert. Then, as the world wobbled on its axis and the climate changed, she speculates that corridors of vegetation opened up and allowed for the dispersal of the earliest human being across the world.

So the migrants who made their way eastwards never really changed their habitation; they merely followed its spread, enjoying

---

[15] *www.haaretz.com/archaeology/genetic-study-finds-new-human-ancestor- 1.5418525*

identical conditions that made possible an identical way of life, until they arrived at the Andaman Islands where they were eventually cut off by the flooding that followed volcanic eruptions, terrifying events they may have carried in their folk memory for ages afterwards.

I find Vanessa Hayes's conclusions exciting because this is familiar territory for me. For years I spent days on end travelling to school in South Africa along the railway line which runs south from the Victoria Falls via Bulawayo into Botswana along the edge of the Kalahari Desert to Mafeking. More recently I have driven the 300 miles from Botswana's second city Francistown to Maun on the edge of the Okavango Delta via the vast almost lifeless Makgadikgadi Salt Pan which tens of thousands of years ago was part of the great wetland, several thousand miles square. It is not easy to imagine it as the birthplace of mankind because it is now so desolate.

Further south is the central Kalahari, given by the British to the Bushmen or San people in 1961. They had been undisturbed until their persecution by both sides following the coincidental arrival in the 1800s of Boers from the south and Bantu from the north. The fact that they dominated a vast area of southern Africa undisturbed for so long, and that they have a genetic relationship with the Andamanese, invites us to compare the culture and lifestyles of both.

The area includes Orapa, the world's biggest open-pit diamond mine, which I visited in 1994 and where I met a young Motswana high-flyer who informed me in no uncertain terms that Bushmen were degenerate and a disgrace to the new Africa. I was shocked at the time, and much more shocked subsequently to learn from John Simpson in his book *Not Quite the World's End* that these brave but gentle people are being forced by the Botswana government out of their lodges and out of the Central Kalahari and into resettlement camps where the loss of their traditional life has led them into total and debilitating dependency. Parallels with the Onge in the Andamans come to mind, not least because of their shared genetic relationship.

I note that Professor Hayes is now studying the culture and lifestyle of the Bushmen of neighbouring north-east Namibia. Her discoveries provide a new reason for redoubled efforts to avoid the threat of extinction for the two remaining viable tribes in the Andaman, the Jarawa and the now even more impressive Sentinelese.

That first view of North Sentinel from 30,000 feet as we flew from Chennai towards Port Blair continues to stick in my mind. The people I met in Port Blair regard it with a kind of awe. It stands so alone, so innocent and so beautiful as it dominates the vast seascape. Of its inhabitants there is no sign and yet they are special: the fiercest, most independent and the most self-sufficient people in the world.

Before the killing of John Chau drew the world's attention to this special place, I had already read about it and seen photographs and maps. It is isolated, pristine and tropical, and covered entirely in thick forest. I also enjoyed imagining my grandfather trying to supervise the census of the Andaman and Nicobar islands more than a hundred years ago, and failing to get any data on the Sentinelese, something for which I now feel grateful. Perversely, perhaps, I also feel grateful that Grandfather's report wrongly labelled the Sentinelese as Jarawa, since it testifies to their secrecy. We still do not have a sample of their DNA, nor do we know the size of their current population. Is that good? I don't know.

It was the Indian anthropologist Triloknath Pandit, already mentioned, who after qualifying at Delhi University joined the Indian Ministry of Tribal Affairs and in 1966 was posted to Port Blair. Pandit's head was full of romantic ideas about the indigenous Andamanese, fueled by the writings of Radcliffe-Brown, who had described the native Andamanese as 'brave' and 'clever'. Inspired, Pandit could hardly wait to get to know them.

Pandit had planned to start work with the Jarawa on South Andaman but before that, he hatched the idea of making the first contact with the Sentinelese that anyone could remember, in spite of the tribe's reputation for extreme hostility.

Pandit assembled an expeditionary party in Port Blair and in

1967 landed on a beach on North Sentinel, where a police escort deposited gifts including coconuts, bananas and a live pig, while the tribesmen remained hidden in the forest. In his book *The Sentinelese*, he says they remained hidden while the party walked inland to find a village that had been temporarily abandoned—as narrated above. The visitors then withdrew in the boat back towards the reef and awaited developments. What they then witnessed was remarkable. A party of tribesmen emerged from the forest with bows and arrows. Taking stock of the tethered pig, they then slaughtered it and buried it in the sand rather than carrying it back to their camp, as Pandit had hoped. The clear message was that intruders were not welcome and their gifts not wanted. Pandit's party returned to Port Blair and he later wrote of his amazement at the idea of an encounter between 'civilized man' and 'primitive man'.

Three years later an official government survey party installed a plaque on the island, declaring it part of India. Meanwhile Pandit continued to pay visits to North Sentinel, each time bearing gifts which he deposited on the beach. Sometimes there were friendly exchanges, at other times demonstrations of hostility, including occasions when islanders would line up along the beach with their backs towards the visitors and assume a defecating posture. At other times they would make obscene gestures including so called 'swaying of penises'. There are records of European armies behaving similarly in medieval times.

One special visit came in 1974 when Pandit accompanied a National Geographic Society expedition with another armed police escort. It was not without incident. An arrow was fired which wounded the society's documentary director in the thigh, which had the curious effect of making him burst out laughing, which prompted the Society to coin the phrase 'Arrows speak louder than words'.

The big breakthrough for the persistent Pandit came in 1991 when again he arrived with a boatload of gifts, including a quantity of coconuts. This time there was a crowd of men, women and children to greet him and his team. At first he must have been alarmed, but soon saw that the people were unarmed. They approached the boat through the neck-high water in droves, some climbing aboard and helping themselves to coconuts. Pandit and his crew got into the water to greet and embrace the people, but recognized quickly that they would not be allowed to set foot on the beach. He said later that though he was cautious, he was not really worried. He was however threatened by a boy who thought the party was getting too close to the shore. Interestingly and significantly on that visit, people who had jumped onto the boat found a concealed gun but their interest seemed to centre only on the fact that it was made of metal.

That first friendly visit was followed by others, ahead of which the expeditions' crews were always pre-screened for communicable diseases such as measles and flu.

Pandit's tenacity had paid off and he came to deplore the labelling of the Sentinelese as hostile. Seeing things from the islanders' point of view, he is quoted as saying, 'we are the aggressors,' 'we are the ones trying to enter their territory' and 'we should respect their wish to be left alone.' These views continue to be upheld by most people with a concern for the future of the tribe, including the campaigning charity Survival International. It is a tragedy that the same conclusion was not reached over contact with the Jarawa on South Andaman before the arrival of settlers and the construction of the Andaman Trunk Road.

Encouragingly, however, in 1996 the Indian Government banned further visits to North Sentinel, lest the prospect of gift-giving by outsiders become too enticing and encourage attitudes of dependency and entitlement. As a result, T.N. Pandit stopped visiting and and has since retired. He is the only person from the outside world ever to come close to knowing the Sentinelese.

But perhaps the Indian government need not have worried too much that the islanders were becoming too welcoming. There was the 2004 arrow attack on the Indian naval helicopter checking on the welfare of the population after the South-Asian tsunami; and in 2006 a party of fishermen was killed with axes and their bodies placed on stakes facing out to sea. By now the island's reputation could be said to have been fully restored and at this point the Indian Government imposed a three-mile limit around the island to keep intruders away.

North Sentinel's notoriety was enhanced with the murder of the would-be missionary John Chau in November 2018. Whether the event makes it more or less likely that there will be future attempts to breach the blockade is a moot point. The determination of the Sentinelese to resist invaders seems undimmed and it appears that the Indian government and the beleaguered tribe are allies in a new-found determination to keep the world away.

That we therefore remain ignorant of these very special people is frustrating, because there is much that we could learn from them. Nevertheless, they must be left alone if there is any chance of their being saved from us and from extinction. For now we should see it as fortuitous that we still have none of their DNA. Long may the Indian government continue in its commitment to keeping us away. Hope arises too from a growing awareness across the world of the importance of human conservation. Surely the awareness will grow and spread that a remnant human population has been discovered who look, think and behave like our earliest human ancestors and that saving them must be right at the top of world conservation priorities.

Given the absence of settlers and tourists, there must be more hope for the Sentinelese than for the Jarawa. They remain critically vulnerable, however, because of their small numbers—or one presumes so: but maybe their numbers are just right. Contributing to the debate on numbers, T.N. Pandit worries about whether the tribe can reproduce at just the right rate for its culture and lineage to last. Interviewed by the journal *Down to Earth* he tells of his 1967 visit when his party walked a kilometre inland and counted 18 huts in a village and when in the 1970s and 80s he saw as many as 30 or 40 people at a time himself. Do these numbers make for a viable population? He fears they do not. Others disagree. One Indian scientist argues that having survived for so long, the question of their future survival can neither be written off nor taken for granted: 'Let nature take its course'. I would not be so cavalier.

I worry also that while it is vital that more be known about the island, the globalization of our interest—the many writings about it, the films made about, the featuring of it on YouTube videos and other social media platforms—must not have a toxic impact on what we wish to protect. While we need a band of supercharged David Attenboroughs to help awaken, inspire and orchestrate world attention, we must not make the same mistakes we have made in the past and become a feature of the Sentinelese' consciousness. With the Indians in the lead, and other governments and international organizations in support, we have to be invisible to them, as they have always wanted.

Chapter 16

The Jarawa in Modern Times

What we have learned from colonial experience in the Andamans is that we learn nothing. Before, during and after Reggie's 22 years in the Andamans, the tribal problem was ignored, sidelined, overshadowed, misunderstood and mishandled in so many ways that there seems never to have been a proper apprehension of what the interests of the tribespeople were, or how their needs could be enshrined, given the pressure from other competing interests that were easier to satisfy and more immediately rewarding.

By the beginning of the twentieth century the northern tribes were all on the verge of extinction and Grandfather Reggie predicted that the Onge and the Jarawa would soon follow. Yet he failed to recognize that the Jarawa's hostility was a survival instinct, that overtures of friendship would lead to its demise, that attempts at education would be destructive and that punishment and reprisals were both pointless and cruel. Except for the limited medical facilities at Kadamtala on Middle Andaman, to which the injured or ill might occasionally be sent, nothing that we did had any impact and the Jarawa were blamed for not being able to take advantage of modernity, and yet we persisted in our futile efforts to civilize and impress.

After Indian independence, settlers from the mainland started to arrive, attracted by large areas of pristine and more or less empty land and were allowed to settle in what had always been Jarawa territory. As already observed, many of these people were ex-servicemen and they were joined by others from other parts of India and refugees from the new Pakistan and Burma. As some of the new settlements were adjacent to Jarawa villages or hunting areas, problems soon arose between the new settlers and the tribesmen.

T.N. Pandit arrived in 1966. Two years later, while based in Port Blair, he had a stroke of luck. He was able to study three captured

Jarawa teenagers and then return them to their tribal habitat laden with gifts for their community. There followed six years of silence when he paid visits to the Jarawa tribal areas without eliciting a response. Then one day, out of the blue, he was greeted by a friendly group. After that he visited them every two weeks or so. He describes how they would take liberties such as stripping off his clothes and poking fingers in his eyes. The effect of these contacts on him was profound. He remembers with reverence and delight how he once witnessed a young Jarawa girl who was watching proceedings from a boat 'with such poise and dignity, as if she was Queen Victoria'. He added that 'you don't need clothes to be dignified.'

Indian policy in the 1970s and 80s towards the Jarawa as well as the Sentinelese was still based on the idea of encouraging interaction by giving gifts, something Pandit clearly understood, as if the handing over of trinkets offset the grabbing of land, the growing incursions of tourists and the structural realignment of the Andaman Trunk Road, the ATR, through the heart of their country.

The authorities also seemed to think that the approach adopted towards the by-now friendly Onge was the model and that it was only a matter of time before the more uncompromising Jarawa let down their guard and proved equally amenable. It was still not recognized that the Onge model was failing. Onge numbers were now down to just over 100 and increasingly they were confined to just a small area in the south of the only island they now inhabited, Little Andaman. There they were provided with government-built huts which they occupied but did not sleep in. They continued to live partly in accordance with their ancient traditions, killing fish with bows and arrows and collecting crabs and other sea creatures, but as the island filled up with settlers, their hunting came to an end. Currently they do little but sit around. In Africa, by curious coincidence, many Bushmen are settled in camps surrounded by the benefits of civilization, and laid on by a government—Botswana— whose very benevolence is erasing the culture it should be trying to preserve.

For the Jarawa, the arrival of settlers in the post-independence days opened up a new era of conflict. The tribe was particularly upset by outsiders occupying areas they had always considered their own domain and were particularly incensed by newcomers who went hunting—a direct challenge, as they saw it, to their own monopoly. Relations got off to a bad start when the Jarawa made retaliatory raids on settler crops. Despite new bush police camps set up to protect both sides, there then followed a succession of killings of settlers and forest workers, but these must have seemed futile even to the Jarawa who since the early years of the century had begun to migrate from Rutland Island at the southern tip of South Andaman across the water to South Andaman and particularly the south west near Port Blair from where the Andaman Trunk Road runs first south via the airport, then north through Middle and North Andaman.

One has to wonder how much thought was given by the Indian Government to the likely consequences of the arrival of settlers on the erstwhile tribal land on South Andaman. There was always bound to be conflict. It seems to me that the decision on settlement was ill considered and and that no heed was taken of accumulated experience. To say that it shows wishful thinking is to be unduly generous to the authorities; more realistically it calls into question the coherence of the Indian government's commitment to the tribes. Could not the new settlers have been confined to Middle and North Andaman, and to outer islands such as Havelock Island, 50 miles away, part of Ritchie's Archipelago, with its tempting diving sites and coral reefs?

Construction on the new road from Port Blair up to the north of North Andaman was approved by the local authority in 1970. Inevitably it ran through or near areas of South Andaman that the Jarawa considered their own. Construction workers started to be attacked and killed but construction continued until the Indian Supreme Court intervened and ordered it to be stopped. Before long however, work was allowed to proceed again, after assurances by the Andaman authorities that tribal interests would be protected. The road was completed in 1989.

Meanwhile, in 1974, although conflict between the Jarawa and the settlers continued, the government tried to achieve peace with a new approach. It involved a contact team from the Tribal Welfare Department revisiting the 'mainstreaming' policy with which the British had flirted. Against anthropological advice, it sought to introduce modern medicine to the Jarawa, ignoring the tribe's own indigenous medical system. Alongside this came a policy, also tried by the British, of buying Jarawa goodwill with gifts. This meant yet more food as well as red cloth and pieces of metal to be fashioned into arrowheads. The unintended consequence was to divert the Jarawas' attention from the bounty of the forests to the bounty of the settlers. As a result they started stealing from settler villages and gardens to supplement their diet. As more settlers arrived, more gardens were planted with more vegetables, bananas and coconuts. These foods were not indigenous to the Andamans and therefore not part of the Jarawa traditional diet, but before long the aboriginals developed a taste for them and stepped up their night-time raids. This became a vicious circle, with attempts to buy peace and harmony leading to more theft and a greater sense of entitlement.

This attitude is illustrated by an incident in 1974 involving a small steamer the MV *Milale* which was carrying a contact team with food and other gifts to Kadamtala. An impatient crowd of young Jarawa swam to the ship before it had docked and started quarrelling over the gifts. Besides dancing on the deck, they pulled at the contact team's clothes. The team included a distinguished female anthropologist who was most upset. Following the incident, the Tribal Welfare Department stopped sending females on contact missions to the Jarawa but did not stop sending its missions.

In 1989, with the completion of the ATR, a new problem arose: the arrival of busloads of tourists all keen to see an aboriginal. In compliance with the law, the buses travelled in groups and were escorted by police, but would stop to allow tourists to photograph tribespeople gathered along the road, even though photography was not officially accommodated. Often, biscuits were swapped for a bow and arrows. In the face of such hypocrisy and its malign effects on the Jarawa, in 2002 the Indian Supreme Court ordered the closure of the road. Again the order was not complied with—again, presumably, because local assurances were given that tribal interests would be looked after. If attempts were made to reinforce the ban on photography, they failed. Tourists brought money to the islands and their demands were paramount. If tourists wanted to photograph islanders, their interests had to be accommodated.

The more the Jarawa were exposed to settlers and onlookers, the more susceptible they became to disease, drugs and alcohol. Stories started to surface also of young girls being bribed with food to dance, and of children to do handstands, and of policemen being bribed to look away while photography and filming took place.

Opinions differ as to when attitudes to this exploitation and abuse began to change. In his book *The Jarawas of the Andamans*, Dr Kar writes of what he sees as a turning point in 1997 after he had been appointed to take charge of the 100-year-old Kadamtala Health Clinic, which by now had come to be accepted by the Jarawa. Kar describes a Jarawa night raid on a settler village when the raiders were driven off. The next morning the barking of a dog drew the villagers' attention to a Jarawa boy of about 14 who was lying in great pain with a badly broken leg, having caught his foot in the roots of a tree. They handed the youth to the police who, fearful of a Jarawa raid to rescue him, transported him quickly by road to the hospital where his leg was operated on and put in plaster. He was given a VIP ward with radio and TV.

Members of the public keen to see a tribesman for the first time now rushed to the hospital where they presented a problem for the police. At first the youth, whose name was Enmi, was terrified as he thought he was going to be killed. He damaged his plaster and refused to eat. Eventually, however, the hospital kitchen cooked a whole fish which was presented to him and which he devoured hungrily. From then on he made progress, getting used to wearing clothes, learning to use the toilet, and leaning a few words of Hindi. He became friendly and communicative, even learning the names of hospital staff and doctors. After five weeks Enmi was discharged and was dropped back by the police at Lakera Lungta, where his father and other Jarawa who thought he had been killed by the *enen* (civilized people) were surprised to see him. He told them his story.

Dr Kar recounts how a year passed; then one day the settlers of the coastal village of Uttara, a couple of miles south of the hospital, on the narrow channel that separates Middle Andaman from South Andaman, saw the mangroves across the bay suddenly quivering. Yet there was no wind! It was Emmi and his friends, three boys and three girls. On being informed, the police went to collect the group, all of whom appeared terrified except for Enmi. They were welcomed by the villagers and offered bananas and coconuts.

Since then, writes Dr Kar, 'exchange of compassion and goodwill started between civilized society and the oldest living tribe in the world.' Not many days later, 70 Jarawa swam across the bay to Uttara and, through gestures, showed that they were hungry. The villagers responded by arranging gifts for them. After that, the whole Kadamtala area arranged boatloads of gifts.

Dr Kar sees this as a positive change, 'when the naked primitive tribe of the hostile Jarawa surrendered their hostility to the world'. Others might see the event differently, as the moment when the Jarawa started finally to be compromised, bringing to an end their 100,000-year culture.

Dr Kar writes of the way the growing understanding between settlers and tribespeople developed as he settled into his new post at Kadamtala. Not long after what he regards as the first peaceful, even joyous, contacts came an incident when he was in a boat with 17 Jarawa. It was stopped by 23 more Jarawa—men women and children—who wanted to board it. As the boat was in danger of being capsized, the doctor and his crew threw the cargo of clusters of bananas into the sea and pushed the would-be boarders overboard as well. He says he feared for a young woman with a baby, but he need not have worried as, with her baby on her back, she swam strongly with the others to a nearby island. What worried him and his small crew was that several Jarawa were armed with bows and arrows; what consoles him now is that the incident ended happily, without attack, when the crew was able to rescue the boat and get it back to the shore. The Jarawa were not frightened any more.

The doctor goes on to describe his life living and working beside the Jarawa, and of the visits that followed in later years. During this time, he built up the warmest relations with the people, and gained an understanding and admiration for them that was unique, making him perhaps their most articulate advocate. The fact remains that all was far from well. Though peace had broken out, by the doctor's reckoning, armed tribesmen continued to raid food and clothes from the settlers and remained deeply disturbed by the incursions of settler hunting parties. In one case a member of a Jarawa raiding party trod on and killed a settler baby sleeping in the corner of a hut. Kar treats this as an accident. Perhaps it was.

Meanwhile the doctor was building a relationship with the Jarawa that gave him unique influence. So confident did he feel in their presence that he was able to confiscate goods that they stolen. On one occasion he managed to retrieve a digital watch stolen from a tourist by convincing the thief that another watch with hands that moved indicated that the one he had stolen was dead.

In another incident on the ATR, tribesmen stopped a vehicle and stole a large number of candles. The doctor accompanied the police to the nearby Jarawa village where they found 70 people holding candles and dancing. He was able to get them to move away by persuading them of the presence of evil spirits of people killed on the road.

Again on the ATR, in October 2000, a group of youths stopped a vehicle carrying the visiting West Bengal minister of tribal welfare. The youths were armed with bows and arrows and, somehow realizing that a tribal welfare escort would not want to intervene, they stole a suitcase full of the minister's clothes. The next month, down at the coast at Lakera Lungta, a boat that was about to sail to Kadamtala with a tribal welfare officer, was boarded by a large group of Jarawa and started to sink. The crew managed to beach it, despite one of the youths throwing the tiller into the sea. He and another youth fired arrows at the fleeing crew members, leaving the tribal welfare officer behind. The situation was rescued by Jarawa women who came to the officer's rescue. Things calmed down despite more youths who had been hunting nearby wanting to beat up those who had fired the arrows. Again the women intervened and the incident was diffused with apologies from the errant youths.

A month later, in December, twenty-five Jarawa entered a village intending to loot. This time the settlers stood up to them. A skirmish ensued and the settlers surrounded the intruders and started to beat them with sticks, injuring several. The tribesmen accepted defeat and those who needed medical treatment were taken to Kadamtala hospital, but remained unrepentant.

Not all the incidents described by the Doctor involved conflict. There was the old settler woman who became disorientated and wandered into the jungle where she got lost. Hungry and thirsty, she was traced by the local Jarawa who rescued her, gave her food and water and sent word to her village that she was well.

By now, after several years, the Jarawa had become reliant on Kadamtala hospital and had total trust in it. Then came the day when a Jarawa patient, a young man called Ohame, died there. It was the hospital's first ever Jarawa death and it came as a great shock to the tribespeople, who believed that all who attended the hospital were cured. The doctor and the tribal welfare department were worried about how the news of the death would be received by the deceased's family and aware that they had to handle it with great care. They gathered at Kadamtala to travel by boat to Spike Island where the family lived. After waiting for a planned police escort that did not turn up, they set off without it, in some trepidation as Spike Islanders had a reputation for shooting arrows at fishermen.

The news of Ohame's death was conveyed first to his mother who gave a great wail and was immediately surrounded by women trying to console her. At that point the party was convinced that arrows would start flying. However Dr Kar managed to calm the islanders and told them that Ohame's body would be delivered for disposal the next day.

When the coffin containing the body arrived it was opened so that the mother, now perfectly composed, could look at her son's face. The body was then laid in the traditional way between the big exposed roots of a tree and covered with branches, heavy logs and stones, giving the visiting party their first chance to observe Jarawa funeral rites.

In spite of these engagements it was becoming harder for the police to deal with the tribesmen, many of whom had become increasingly demanding and disrespectful of settlers' property. What is more, when thwarted they were not afraid to vent their fury, and such were the political sensitivities about the Jarawa that the police were under strictest orders not to open fire, even with blanks, even under the greatest provocation. In November 2001 a small group of Jarawa visited a police post at Colinpur Beach, on a bay to the west of South Andaman. The police gave the tribesmen food and asked them to leave but the tribesmen demanded a boat to take them back to their huts. When the police refused, the Jarawa caused considerable damage before leaving. They returned two days later to cause further damage and fired arrows, fortunately without hurting anybody.

The next month a team of officers from the local Andamese authority and the government of India met to carry out research and assess Jarawa problems and grievances. The idea was for the team, which included Dr Kar, to live beside a Jarawa village for a month at a place called Hieulele Chadda. The party was dropped off in the evening and welcomed by the local women and children, who helped unload their camping gear and erect tents. They were particularly pleased that Dr Kar, who had accompanied the team, promised to dispense medicines and medical care to the village during the stay.

In the evening Kar fell asleep but was woken by what he describes as two giant, naked, Jarawa men who had returned from a hunting expedition. In what he describes as another turning point in relations with the Jarawa, he was welcomed by the men who recognized him. They assured him of all help and security. Lying awake in his tent, with the tune of a song sung by the village children still ringing in his ears, he mused on how beautiful and enjoyable was the life of these Jarawa.

During the month-long stay the party visited several parts of South and Middle Andaman and one day walked for eight hours eastwards towards the ATR, crossing a number of streams and hills. At one point a Jarawa youth suddenly climbed a tree and from a groove took out a skull and brought it down. It had belonged to one of his ancestors and was placed according to custom in a secret place. The youth handed it to Dr Kar who kept it for craniometry.

Most touchingly revealing are Kar's recollections of a televised World Cup football match in June 2002 between Sweden and Senegal which patients in the hospital were able to watch. He says the joy of the Jarawa knew no bounds on seeing the black Senegalese scoring a goal and they danced in front of the television set.

He also regarded as promising an incident in March 2003 when a party of settlers was caught hunting in tribal territory by Jarawa youths who overpowered them and tied them to trees with a creeper. They then sent for tribal welfare officers who rushed to the area where the hunters were being held, expecting to find that they had been killed. Instead they had been spared and released having, Kar hopes, learned their lesson.

The doctor describes his last day living among the Jarawa and his transfer back to Port Blair. He was particularly moved to be invited to the hut of a Jarawa man, Oiham, who took him down to the sea shore, sat him on a pile of freshly cut branches covered in leaves, and gave him a special meal of delicious jungle fruits. After the meal he boarded his boat and when he looked back after some time, he saw the naked Jarawa who had come to wish him farewell still standing on the shore, waving goodbye.

For 20 years Dr Ratan Chandra Kar played a crucial role as a go-between, acquiring status among the Jarawa as an outsider to be respected. In the early days when he visited Jarawa encampments, the police used to provide him with an escort. After that, he says, he won enough trust to go on his own and never felt at risk.

On one occasion in October 2008 bad weather forced him to anchor his boat and seek shelter at a nearly Jarawa settlement. He tells how he entered a hut he had not realized was exclusively used by widows and adolescent unmarried girls, and from which males were banned. The women and girls were puzzled initially but then recognized and started to entertain him. When the storm was over and the time came to leave, one particularly charming and beautiful young woman invited him to come and visit her in her hut on his next visit. He never took her up on her offer. One day, he recalls, the woman asked him affectionately if he was well. Now, he says, the girl has married a brave hunter and is leading a happy, conjugal life.

Dr Kar marvels at the growing warmth that he saw developing between aboriginal tribespeople and civilized society, of which he was the main representative. But I think we need to put his more homey anecdotes on one side, however compelling they may be, and take stock of how the Jarawa are coping with their new reality now he is not there to intercede.

It seems to me that despite all the stories of mutual goodwill, the conclusions are almost entirely negative. In short, the Jarawa have no agency. Deeply antipathetic to the arrival of settlers and tourists about which they can do virtually nothing, they now concentrate on taking advantage of them, which from their point of view includes the right to help themselves to their possessions. This is not simply the equivalent of their going hunting for wild pig in the forest or foraging for roots; it is a crude, resentful but completely understandable type if redistributive justice, a wish to get something back from new colonizers who have invaded their territory and are having a better time of it. Growing resentment, frustration, anger and a depth of psychological disturbance we can only begin to guess at arise from a degradation of their former independence and integrity and it originates from our sapping of their ability to determine their own fate. Would it help them if they could see and understand what is happening to the Onge?

The fact is that the future of the Jarawa and their way of life has been dashed by the priority given to the needs of incomers, the seemingly relentless determination of the local Andaman authority to construct and then exploit the Andaman Trunk Road, and the inability of India to find a way of settling rival claims fairly and decisively. Behind this, the mile upon mile of seemingly empty land, the fertility of the soil and the easy access to good hunting has been overwhelmingly attractive to former landless refugees and other settlers. The potential of coral sand, a pristine environment and everything else the Andamans have to offer foreign tourists is also set to open up economic opportunities for locals and overseas investors that few will be able to resist or manage.

The Andaman Trunk Road is the most obvious provocation on account of the daily expectation it raises of easy returns. Dr Kar is as upset by this as anyone and has written of his anger at how the Jarawa are aroused and toyed with. He tells of an occasion when Jarawa women, having been refused food by tourists, snatched babies, apparently intending to take them into the jungle. When he was asked to investigate, he interceded with the women who told him there had been a misunderstanding and that they merely wanted to cuddle the babies. It is difficult to reconcile this explanation with the tourists' understandable outrage at having their children stolen, but it is equally difficult not to sympathize with the women's helplessness, and the predicament they are put in by being peered at like circus animals and expected to perform.

In short, we do not know what emotions the Jarawa experience as they wait for the convoys to appear or what the women's motivation truly was on the day of the snatching. My mother's early experiences convinced her of the tribespeople's capacity for love and affection on family visits to the islands. The incident of Jarawa women on the ATR merely snatching babies 'so we could cuddle them' may not be so far-fetched as we imagine.

In the years after Dr Kar's departure from Jarawa country, incidents along the Andaman Trunk Road multiplied as ever-increasing numbers of tourists paid coach companies and taxis good money to show them the sights. The authorities imposed rules which, besides the banning of photography, included bans on stopping on the road, communicating with the Jarawa, giving them food and presents and offering exchanges. The rules are impossible to enforce, however, and so are largely ignored; bus drivers, for example, have no commercial interest in enforcing them, and tourists now know that if they take biscuits and other goods on board the coaches with them, there is every chance of their returning to their hotels at the end of the day with Jarawa booty: bows and arrows or jungle honey and resin.

It is not only the ATR that has proved vexatious. There have been problems to the west of South Andaman in the Tirrur area—once remote but now accessible by National Highway 11 which terminates there. The Jarawa in this region remained hostile but continued to steal bananas and coconuts from settler gardens. The settlers took the view that the Jarawa were doing this because they were hungry and demanded that the authorities provide them with free food.

In reality, however, the Jarawa Reserve extended to 1,000 square miles and contained all the food that the tribespeople could possibly need. The settlers were making the problem worse for both sides by being too ready to find a solution that tried to paper over the resentment caused by their own presence. Though the authorities were at first slow to recognize the danger of such a practice, tribal affairs department staff were subsequently instructed to deter gift-giving were possible, though without exploring more satisfactory remedies.

Sometimes there are more dangerous clashes between settlers and Jarawa. In one incident north of Middle Andaman, a troop of Jarawa children swam out to ask some fishermen to give them fish. The fishermen refused and poured hot water on the children. On hearing the children's cries, a Jarawa man swam out to the fishing boat and started to fight with the fishermen. In the clash he killed a fisherman and was himself then wounded and drowned.

Over time, the danger posed by the ATR, settlers and tourism has attracted negative attention from outside bodies such as Survival International. There has also been lobbying from local groups concerned by the reputational damage to their community by treating the Andamans as a safari park for 'primitive' aboriginals as if they were simply an exotic species.

The overwhelming tragedy, however, is that even where the Andaman and Indian government authority have taken steps to mitigate clashes, these are seen largely in local terms as conflicts between different groups with different interests. No one seems to be thinking in terms of mankind's history and of the disappearance of a way of life that, until we arrived, was better able to withstand threats, and over a longer period, than any other example of humanity on our planet.

My recent visit to the Andamans confirms my impression that the enormous interest in the Jarawa people is not in any way related to saving them or learning from them. For the hundreds of tourists arriving daily from the mainland at Port Blair, the main objective is simply to see them, and so great is the traffic that Jarawa-tourism has generated that the airport is now being expanded. As for the ordinary settler community, the Jarawa remain a background issue that only comes to their attention when written about in the papers. During my trip I only met three people who had ever seen one. Two were the middle-class Indian couple who told me of the bus driver who had given biscuits to a Jarawa youth on the ATR while warning the passengers that they were not allowed to. The other was Denis Giles, the newspaper editor, who had travelled up the ATR in its early days to visit Kadamtala. While there, he came across a group of young Jarawa who happened to be visiting for the first time. Alone and terrified, he stood stock still while three Jarawa girls approached him and checked him out, first below, then above, and then apparently concluded that he was human and male. None of the staff members of the tribal welfare office I spoke to in Port Blair had seen a Jarawa. None are to be seen on the streets of Port Blair, none are employed in the town, none are educated, none can read. Even in their 'in-between' state, none is rushing to embrace whatever modernity they have come across in us. In the one case on record of the young Jarawa, Enmi, who was given such an opportunity after being hospitalized at Kadamtala, he opted without hesitation to return to his life in the forests as a hunter-gatherer.

That is not to say that the settler community is immune to their concerns, nor is it true that the loudest voices urging the Indian

Government to take more effective steps to close the ATR and protect the Jarawa from civilization are all foreign. But there is no sign that the problem is being tackled with urgency or with the kind of drastic measures that are needed and that would disadvantage those who currently call the shots.

The situation is not helped by key government staff not staying long enough in the islands to gain a thorough understanding of the issues or by the central government's failure to come down hard on Andamanese officialdom, which until now has seems to flout all sanctions as it sees fit. It is, admittedly, a complicated and delicate situation but no one has yet emerged from it with credit. The Indian government's reactions have looked erratic, uncommitted and duplicitous. The prevention of Erika Hagelberg from visiting the Onge to collect a DNA sample after getting authorization from Delhi, for example, smacked of confusion and suggested that central and local government policies were out of step. This impression is reinforced by the chaotic history of the ATR and the surrender to short-term economic interests. To counter impressions of indifference, India needs to intervene now to save the situation from deteriorating further.

India's official stance is protective, particularly since an international conference on the Andaman tribes in 2004. And yet what I saw on Havelock Island looked haphazard and uncontrolled, with forest being cleared to make way for houses, gardens and plantations. North Sentinel has been ring-fenced but in most of the rest of the islands it looks like a potential free-for-all. This is not just bad for the indigenous islanders but for the entire population. If forest clearance were to take place across the islands, the Andamans' unique environment would lose the very qualities that make it so appealing as a tourist destination. Currently long stretches of new roads look like the suburbs of New Zealand.

Can there be a future for tourism and the Jarawa? The people I spoke to in the Andamans think there can, but not without extremely tough decisions over land use. In my own view, mainstreaming and happy coexistence are wishful thinking and cannot be the answer. In the recent case of an infant born to a Jarawa woman who was killed because it was light skinned, details of the crime were forwarded to the tribal welfare department for deliberation. Among Andaman residents, opinion was divided. A local activist, Samir Acharya, wanting to play down the situation, told the *New York Times* that the Jarawa had every right to maintain the purity of its race. The police superintendent, Atul Kuma Thakur, countered that nobody was above the law. Commenting on the case, the *Andaman Chronicle* wrote:

> The Jarawa have their own systems and traditions which they have followed for centuries. Is it the right time to interfere? That is the question.

That is indeed the question and solving it will be tough. In this situation the Indian government deserves international under-standing and help as do Indian and local lobbying groups. Answers are needed that satisfy all, but we need them now.

There is little comfort to be taken from our belated attempts to save the tiger and the black rhino from extinction. These are easy targets. We have largely failed in our attempts to tackle climate change and the global crisis. while deforestation in Borneo and the Brazilian rain forest continue apace with governmental approval. If it seems inappropriate to be comparing aboriginal humans with animals, trees and coal reserves, we can at least tantalise ourselves with our failure to have done very much in those respects either.

One key decision could break the logjam for the Jarawa: the closure of the ATR. From this, much else would follow, notably the relocation of some or all the settlers or, less attractively, the moving of the Jarawa to areas where they might have a better chance of living undisturbed. For any of this there would have to be an intermediaries as well-schooled as Dr Ratan Chandra Kar in tribal attitudes, and in negotiations with the settler community, and committed to saving the unique human legacy that is the Jarawa.

What does not assist this ambition is the argument either that the Jarawa's identity is now irretrievable or that their best option is to live alongside us. Kar writes passionately about the harm done by the construction of the ATR but does not see contact between settlers and tribespeople as equally damaging. He may be right to accept the settlers' presence as a *fait accompli*, but is surely wrong to presume that we and they can co-exist without total loss of who and what they are. Kar's view that all plans and programmes will fail 'if you are not able to share the sorrows and sufferings of the Jarawa' is surely mere sentimentality. We do not want to tame the Jarawa or treat them like pets; they need their anger and defiance and they deserve to be separate. We can watch them from a distance—and indeed we should, because they probably present the only chance mankind now has for exploring the complexities of human evolution. Besides answering questions about our progress over the past 100,000 years, the Jarawa are the key to our understanding the very basics of how we operate. If we want to understand the way in which the human mind, on its own and in social groups, has developed its ideas about self-protection, instinct, survival, health, relationships, language, music, self-governance, property, conflict and its avoidance, sexuality, adolescence and happiness, we still have the Jarawa as a test case. But not if we sacrifice them, domesticate them, engage with them, abuse them, exploit them, befriend them, and make them dependent on us.

Currently the Jarawa are heading for a state of supine dependency, like the Onge of Little Andaman, and we cannot want them also to slide into such terminal decline. We can only protect them by cutting them off from ourselves. There are still communities such as those from the conservative Tirrur area that stick firmly to tribal traditions, avoid contact with outsiders and continue their hunter-gatherer life unadulterated. If there are others who, in the view of some, are convinced that the Jarawa are a lost cause, then the Tirrur contingent may be the core of those whom we conserve, able to play a vital part in bringing the tribe as a whole back to a way of life that saves them. After all, the dangers they now face are relatively new and Jarawa tradition is massively old. If we can only take ourselves out of their picture, they might survive our assault on them.

In some ways it is encouraging that our relations with the Jarawa are still fairly distant. Dr Kar must have known tribespeople better than any other outsider but even he only talked about two individuals: the young woman who invited him to her hut and the villager who entertained him to a special farewell meal of jungle fruits. We still have not got to know the Jarawa at a personal level. I have come across no account of any individuals or opinions from Radcliffe-Brown, grandfather or T.N. Pandit. The nearest I came was the very general assessment from grandmother Bessie, quoted earlier, who described them as quick and intelligent, keen on sport and attractive to the European. That suggests that there is still a real distance between us and them. In some ways that is encouraging.

We cannot read their minds. If we knew them better, we might better understand how they see the world and what their own ambitions are, if they have ambitions. We assume they want to be left alone; we may wrongly assume that they do not want what we have already shown them. We know they want our medical help, just as much as they want our coconuts and bananas. They do learn, but not necessarily what we have wanted them to learn.

This leaves us with a huge moral problem. If we wish to cut the Jarawa off from us, we must do so in the knowledge that we are also putting up a barrier against their ability to learn from us and change —in short, to evolve, if contact with us is evolution. In that sense, our wish to protect them is not just a recognition of their unique value but of our own self-disgust. In wanting them to be them, we want them not to be us.

Making decisions such as these has nasty overtones of playing God—and God, too, wanted Adam and Eve not to be like Him. Although I have seen how African tribes have welcomed change, I have also seen how the Onge have been brought down by it and how the Great Andamanese were destroyed by it. 'Civilisation' is a heavy burden, too heavy for those unprepared for it—too heavy, possibly, for us too. Yet we stand at a point where we are being required to make life and death choices: how to determine the Jarawa's future and how to determine our own. Whatever we now do or do not do, we will be shaping how and whether they survive. Applying our intelligence and compassion to their fate at least seems manageable when compared to applying it to ourselves.

It must surely be a major consideration of those involved in the tourist bonanza that the Jarawa are currently being changed and corrupted by a dreadful, humiliating slide towards dependency and the loss of a life that they love and value above all else and that has sustained them since mankind began. As our contact with them becomes more insidious and corrosive, an increasing number of prosecutions are reported in the *Andaman Chronicle* for the sexual exploitation of Jarawa girls through alcohol and drugs. Is that what we want our legacy of contact with the Jarawa to be remembered for?

Until now the Indian Government has been dissuaded from taking necessary action by vested interests and the short-termism of local civil servants who lack experience, commitment and depth of understanding. India can surely be persuaded to take the steps needed to put into practice the policies to which it is committed, without making the damaging concessions that have let the settler community off the hook too many times in the past. If they do, they will have stood up to the worst pattern in human history: that of the destruction of the weak by the strong. India now has the opportunity to do an extraordinary thing: to give life to the most vulnerable. Here is a group of humans who have endured longer and more tenaciously in their original form than any others of our species, but whom in just a few years we have transformed by our selfishness and stupidity into the most fragile. What a boast it would be if India could launch them on another 100,000 years. I dare to hope.

A plea

If you have been moved by anything I have said in this book, may I invite you to visit the website of *Survival International*, read what it says about the Jarawa, and then use the site to send a pre-worded email petition to Shri Munda, India's current Minister of Tribal Affairs, and to Admiral Joshi, the Lieutenant Governor of the Andaman and Nicobar Islands and Vice Chairman of the Islands Development Agency. The petition says:

> I am extremely concerned about the Jarawa tribe of the Andaman Islands. Every day hundreds of tourists travel along the Andaman Trunk Road in the hope of 'spotting' members of the Jarawa tribe— treating the Jarawa like animals in a safari park. The Supreme Court of India ordered in 2002 that the road should be closed, yet it remains open. I urge you to ban tourists from travelling on the road through the Jarawa's land and ensure that they use the alternative sea route instead. I also urge that the Jarawa be allowed to make their own decisions about their future, in their own time.

I thoroughly endorse this message. I hope you will too.

Appendices

Appendix 1
A Jungle Experience
by Elizabeth Coldstream
The Ladies' Field
21 November 1903

There are few persons who have spent a week under canvas in fine weather, be it anywhere in the world, who would not gladly spend those days over again; and when that week is spent on one of the best shooting-grounds of India, in the middle of a vast expanse of forest, with genial companions, few, indeed, are the pleasures which surpass it.

My sister E. and I had come to pay a visit to our uncle, Major W., who was in civil employ, and most thoroughly did we enjoy the camp life after the occupations and social enjoyments of our life in Simla.

We had left Blankpur some days before, and now it lay about forty miles to the east of us. Rising ere the sun had shown himself over the low hills on the horizon, we had left our one-night camp daily, halting only for Sunday.

The tents were always pitched under a group of large banyan trees, and very glad we were to get into the shade; for the Indian sun can be unpleasantly warm even at 8 a.m. during the cold season. Our useful little native maid, who with the cook and the tents and various servants, always went on ahead of us, would have everything ready and, after a hot bath and breakfast, we would feel as fresh as possible.

A runner came from Blankpur every day bringing our letters, vegetables and flowers, and when the latter had been arranged and the cook interviewed we would spend the day in reading, writing or sketching, and perhaps music (for a small American organ was always with us), till it was time to go out for a stroll on the elephants in the cool of the evening.

And so we had spent some days and now had reached Chandgarh, a village on the borders of the Nepal forests. Here we had arranged to spend Christmas week, and hoped to have some big-game shooting; not that E. and I handled rifles, but we enjoyed accompanying the sportsmen. At Chandgarh we were joined by two friends of our uncle, Colonel B. and Mr. F., and by a cousin of our own, Mr. Grant.

On arrival at this camp we found plenty to do in arranging our large square dining tent and a smaller sitting one with ever-greens and pictures, and very pretty and cheery we made it look for Christmas, I assure you. Just as we were finishing breakfast on the day of our arrival at Chandgarh, while we were anxiously awaiting the latest news from the forests as to whether there were any signs of tigers about, one of our native guard came up and, salaaming to my uncle, said a man had brought news from the jungle. The *shikari*[16] was ordered to come up at once and give his report. He said a young buffalo belonging to a village herd had that morning been killed, and that they had tracked the tiger into a patch of thick jungle about three miles distant from our camp. His story sounded most encouraging, and we felt that tiger had not long to live. So orders were given for the elephants, and for the collection of 200 natives to act as beaters from the neighbouring villages. The *shikaris*, too, were told how many of us there would be, for as the jungle in that part is very thick the tigers cannot be surrounded by elephants in the usual way, but the sportsmen have to sit perched in trees, twelve to fifteen feet above the ground, on seats roped to strong branches and surrounded by screens of leaves to prevent the tiger from seeing them. These arboreal seats are called *machans*, and if there are more than one they are placed about forty yards apart. Towards these leafy ambuscades the tigers are driven. The beaters start some way back from where the tiger is supposed to be lying; and on either side from the beaters up to the row of *machans* are placed 'stops'—that is, natives up trees—who, if the tiger tries to pass them, make a noise by knocking on the tree, which rarely fails to turn the tiger, who slinks off, and so is kept in the middle till within range of the rifles on the *machans*.

As the beaters had three miles to walk to the hunting-ground we had to give them a long start, and it was nearly noon when our line of elephants left the camp—E. and I riding on one which was renowned for its easy paces. We were armed with branches of the

---

[16] Hindi word for 'hunter'.

castor-oil plant, which we found effectual in keeping off flies. We also took small light sticks, with a V-fork at the end, with which we kept the branches off our heads while going through thick jungle seated on our tall elephant. On arrival at the *machans* we clambered up as quietly as possible, E. sharing our uncle's seat and I that of my cousin, Mr. Grant. Hardly were we seated when we heard the distant noise of the beaters and knew that the beat had begun, though at a distance from us of many hundred yards through the forest. We knew, too, that the tiger, if he was there, had heard it too, and so we kept a sharp look-out for him. Nearer and nearer came the beating of drums, mingled with the screams of both men and elephants. A noise of galloping to our right, and a grand stag came rushing through the brush-wood. He had magnificent horns, but the noise of a shot would have 'turned' the tiger at once, if he was there, and I confess I was not sorry that the beautiful creature was left to pursue his way in safety. Hardly had he gone when a family of black jungle-pig came trotting under us, evidently not at all approving of being disturbed. By this time the beaters were within two hundred yards of us, and we were getting anxious, when a troop of monkeys came chattering through the branches over our heads, and several peacocks rose majestically with spreading plumage out of the long grass in front of us.

Then we heard a heavy footfall to our left, and the brushwood cracking under a stealthy step, and suddenly there, about sixty yards before us, trotted out a grand full-grown tiger. He seemed to pause a moment, perhaps suspecting something, but he was not left to meditate long. Taking a steady aim Mr. Grant fired, and the report was followed by a roar which seemed to shake the jungle. Trembling with excitement, I jumped up on our seat, to see the tiger lying on his back, struggling to rise and snarling angrily. His back was broken, and another shot ended his career just as the line of beaters came up. There were, of course, great rejoicings, and Mr. Grant was congratulated all round. The elephants were sent for from where they had been stationed during the beat, some few hundred yards off, and, using them as ladders, we got down from our leafy coverts and inspected the beautiful beast, now lying quite dead. He was then roped on to an elephant and so taken to camp. We were all in excellent spirits and quite ready for lunch, which we found waiting for us in a shady spot in the dry bed of a river half a mile from our *machans.*

While we were thus indulging ourselves we were interrupted by one of the native guard galloping up with the news that a leopard had 'killed' about a couple of miles down the river-bed. Orders were given immediately for a *machan* to be put up; and lots were drawn as to who was to go after him. My uncle was the lucky man, so he and I, with a book each and plenty of rugs, started off. When we arrived the *shikaris* were just finishing the preparation of our seat in the middle of a tree, situated just over the spot where, stark and stiff and partially devoured, lay the leopard's prey: Meanwhile, we examined the leopard's footprints, making out that he was a large animal. When the men had done their task and retired to a distance we climbed into our seats from the back of our elephant and settled down for our wait among the branches as quietly as possible, as we suspected our prey was not very far off and it was getting late in the afternoon. The leopard almost invariably returns at sunset to his 'kill' of the previous night. It was a very lovely spot. Our tree overhung the jungle side of the river bed and opposite us rose a steep white cliff, which gradually became a golden red with the light of the setting sun. The sky in the west seemed to be on fire and the colours on the various trees round us were exquisite. Not a breath of air stirred the branches, and the only sound to be heard was the steady cooing of the wood pigeons and an occasional scream from a peacock. We sat for a long time enjoying Nature in this wonderful stillness, not caring to open our books. To my mind there are few things so impressive as the quietness of a vast forest. The short Indian twilight was coming on when a hungry-looking jackal slunk up cautiously and inspected the 'kill'. We sent him off by rustling the leaves. Shortly after a big, ugly hyena came on the scene, and he also was made to retire. The efforts of a rat to carry off the dead goat were amusing us greatly when suddenly he too decamped, and looking up we saw the leopard coming crouching along towards us. When he was about thirty yards off my uncle fired. There was a smothered roar, and in a moment the leopard was coming rolling and tumbling towards our tree. He was evidently hit, but very much alive; and I confess I felt nervous as I saw the fierce creature snarling within a few feet of us, and I expected to see him on our tree every minute, but another shot put the poor beast out of his pain.

In great spirits at having had such a successful day, we shouted for our elephants, which were always within call, my uncle giving a hoarse deer-like bark, which carries far and was the understood signal. Leaving the leopard to be roped on to an elephant we started homewards, and very glad we were when the camp lights came into view after our long day. The rest of the party had got back some hours before.

Appendix 2
A Day in the Nepal Terai
by Elizabeth Lowis
Undated

Sahib—Khubber hai.[17] Inspiriting words to the sportsman[18] in India, especially when he recognizes the voice of a faithful and experienced *shikari*.

We had been encamped in a lovely spot on the borders of Nepal for some days, awaiting news of a tiger.

There were several about and one we particularly wished to secure, as he had been a source of danger to the neighbouring villages during the past year.

The days had been spent pleasantly enough, for a clear fast flowing river ran past our camp in which there was excellent fishing and several *mashers* had already been accounted for.

Every evening too we would enjoy a stroll on the elephants, after partridge, black buck and anything that came in our way along the outskirts of the forest.

Some of our party had been revelling in the beauties of the spot and spent a large part of their time in sketching. But today the news we have waited for had come and we knew it was reliable for Gunga Singh never brought us *khubber*[19] unless he could show us sport.

A very large tiger, he now informed us, was at that moment reposing in a patch of tall grass some 300 yards away, on an island in the bed of a dry river.

He had tracked him himself right into the grass, having first satisfied himself that the tiger had had a very large meal of one of the poor buffalo calves we had tied up in the jungle as bait.

The elephants were ordered at once, all the twenty-five we had out in camp, kindly lent by a neighbouring Rajah.

---

[17] Sir, there's news, in Bengali (Bangla).
[18] In this context, a hunter, especially of tigers.
[19] (Good) news, in Bengali (Bangla).

My share of the arrangements was to see that there would be plenty to eat and drink when we had aged our game, for we have some twelve miles to go first.

Armed with books and rugs, not to mention the rifles and lunch basket, we got on to our pads. The elephants with *howdahs* came too, but they are so uncomfortable when going at any pace that we always used ordinary pads on other elephants till we got close to the game.

Swinging along in the midday sun, our line of huge beasts made the usual sensation, as we hurried through the little villages—and out across the fields till we reached a patch of grass on the river bed just outside a thick jungle.

Here changing elephants and forming line—a couple of guns were sent out on either side and one to the end of the grass to prevent the tiger crossing the sand into the jungle.

Our elephant went through with the rest of the line of beating elephants all close together.

One cannot help admiring the cool way the *mahouts*[20] urge their elephants in after tiger. Both they and the *shikari* who tracked wounded tigers are I think worthy of the greatest admiration and respect for their never-failing pluck and interest in our sport.

Slowly we advanced, the elephants slowly pushing their way through the grass and low trees and seeming to understand as well as we did, the work they had to do.

Suddenly as we got to the middle of the island, just in front of our elephant we heard an angry 'waugh, waugh' and caught a glimpse of the huge yellow beast as he got up sulkily from his midday siesta, very much annoyed at being disturbed.

He slunk through the grass ahead of us to the end where he was turned by a shot that missed him. Lashing his tail as he trotted back towards our line, he had broken through it before we realized he was there.

Back we turned after him, Colonel A. giving him a shot in the flank as he disappeared. This brought him round sharp, and he came for us—ears laid back and mouth open, emitting a series of roars as he bounded through the grass.

The sudden attack was too much for our old elephant, staunch as she had proved herself on many a previous occasion. Swinging short round, so as to throw us violently against the side of the *howdah*,

---

[20] Elephant drivers.

she fled, tail up and trumpeting, the tiger at her heals. In her mad rush through a low clump of trees, we disturbed a nest of bees—and in a moment we were the centre of a cloud of infuriated insects.

Fortunately, in view of such a contingency, we were provided with rugs and I was quickly enveloped in one of these, but peeping out I could see Colonel A. who was standing in front of the *howdah*, his face and hands black with bees.

In spite of this predicament he was able to turn and fire a quick right and left past me into the tiger over the tail of our elephant— rolling him over in his tracks.

It was only just in time, for I could distinctly hear the snarling part of the tiger within a few feet of me, and every moment expected him to land on top of us. Colonel A.'s shot had however most effectually given him his quietus—and as soon as the *mahout* had pulled the elephant up and brought it back, we found him lying quite dead in the grass. Having first satisfied ourselves that he really was dead, we turned off into the thick jungle where we shook off our large following of bees by lighting a fire and smoking them away. This was not accomplished unscathed, Colonel A.'s face and hands being covered with scores of stings and my own to a lesser degree. They proved however to be a mild species of bee, and we suffered little inconvenience from their stings after the first half hour.

While we had been thus employed, the dead tiger had been padded and was now brought up for our inspection. He was a very large and old beast and his skin had some bad scars of recent fights, probably with pigs.

Later when we measured him in camp he proved to be just ten feet, the biggest tiger Colonel A., who had accounted for a great number, had ever shot.

Mounting once more we went off to hunt for our companions for there had been a stampede of the elephants, at the first alarm of 'bees', and while the tiger was keeping us employed, the rest of the line were to be seen careering over the surrounding country— fortunately in the direction of home—which meant open field and not thick jungle.

It was rather a comical sight to see the huge beasts rolling along at a great pace, each of the *mahouts* enveloped in his blankets, head and all, and the unfortunate occupant of the *howdah* or pad waving his arms in self-defence from the stray bees which had left us to follow them.

They soon overtook our party and when we reached a quiet cool spot got down for lunch and enjoyed the rest and refreshment.

On our homeward way we beat through some likely places and were lucky enough to come across leopard, we bagged him after he had led us a long chase, slinking through the grass just ahead of our elephants but barely giving us a glimpse of himself. A couple of florican[21] too were added to the bag.

---

[21] Bird, the small Asian bustard.

Musings of a Magistrate's Wife
by Elizabeth Lowis
1920

Even in the East, where tears are generally nearer the surface, a grown man's sobs cannot be heard without concern and when they came to me that lovely morning in the tropics they woke in me a great sympathy.

Sitting, writing, as I often do, in our large airy verandah, with its grand view of sea and island, the scent of stephanotis and lilies borne to me on the gentle breeze and the whole land and sea scape lying sparkling in the morning sun, I have to either harden my heart or go away to a more distant part of the house.

From that verandah I can see a corner of the little room below where the wooden railed enclosure in front of the raised platform shows that the room is used as a Court and here the local Justice of the Peace administers the Law in the name of the Government. Besides the Court there are also the Police Guard quarters and an open space below the verandah.

I like to think that the masses of flowers and ferns in that stone courtyard may help, if ever so slightly, to rest the criminal's eyes as he waits to hear his fate, handcuffed and attached by rope to the strong arm of the law, in the shape of a large Indian policeman.

The small whitewashed room, its only touch of colour a fine print of H.M the King Emperor, has witnessed many a tragedy and many an aching heart has been relieved, or still further hurt and perhaps hardened by what takes place there, according as to whether the sentence is lighter or heavier than the prisoner has expected. Just, I know it is, at least as far as our present conditions can make it possible for one man to judge another, and knowing as I do, that he who administers it is the soul of honour and has quick sympathies, in such matters.

At this time of change and growth, when men's minds are stretching out to learn new aims and new methods, is it too much to hope that in the near future we may find a better way to help our erring brothers?

He whose sobs I had heard, as he was led out after hearing his sentence, was a small spare Burman with a haggard careworn face and the hopeless look one so often sees in the faces of criminals. He had committed a brutal murder and the evidence was clear, and, unless one takes into consideration that a man is so often at the mercy of a passing strong emotion, no excuse was possible.

The emotional side of a Burman is always uppermost and one can realize how, as the convicts sit working in silence side by side, the thoughts of revenge and hate must grow to be overpowering; there is no relief from this daily torture till even the death sentence seems hardly worth consideration, so long as the short relief which revenge may bring is satisfied.

Such temptations have been yielded to before, at least once or they would not find themselves in their present circumstances. It is this thought and the knowledge that, given the same conditions, and the same childlike impulses, I for one can so easily picture myself in that criminal's place.

This was almost a unique occasion, for whatever the sentence, it is usually heard without visible emotions. The tragedy is enacted times without number and I see and hear nothing, it is only my vivid imagination which fills in the silences with such painful accuracy, though occasionally the murmur of a pleading voice stating his case to the Judge is no uncommon sound. I may hear nothing but the clank of the prisoner's leg irons, as he arrives led up by the Police and the same when he is taken away; that is all I know of the crisis in that prisoner's life.

The old saying of 'Give a man a bad name and you may as well hang him' holds good in many parts and where there are more or less suffering similarly it must be harder to live down. However that may be, there is no doubt that it is done successfully in many cases, and in my own personal experience I have known more than one instance of a man coming to those Penal Isles with a terrible history of crime behind him in his own Province and in an Indian jail and have seen him grow steadily into a useful an self-respecting member of the community, provided and this is a sine qua non, that his is treated with sympathy and given plenty of congenial work.

A man who was known in India as a murderer, a drunkard, a thief and a gambler grew to be ashamed of even a suggestion that he was not altogether upright and has proved himself to be honest and no doubt our belief in him helped him to this position. But when temptation has been too much for a prisoner and he finds himself in that room of momentous memories, whatever his sentence, whether enhancement of his original term of deportation a further period of cellular jail or his release, in the form of the extreme penalty he, as a man is deserving of our sympathy and possibly, some day our developed sense of right, may prevent us from causing a man to cease living because he has sinned.

The True Story of a Floating Shrine
by Elizabeth Lowis
Undated

The most important of the Buddist festivals in Burma is that of
Thadnidyat. This is held at the annual 'Lent' and occurs in October.
The rainy season is generally over by then and the preparations for
this festival are more elaborate than for any other.

Every religious festival in Burma is signalised by offerings made
to the priests and these men, in their picturesque yellow robes and
shaven heads, flock in thousands to the various towns and villages
and receive offerings of every sort.

Arches of bamboo and coloured paper are erected in open spaces,
figures of dragons to guard the entrances and figures of princes and
princesses of grotesque shape are built up by the devout Buddists in
honour of the festival.

In the evenings fire balloons are sent off and illuminated rafts are
set adrift on the sea and rivers. These rafts vary greatly in size and
importance but the general appearance is of a miniature temple
pagoda.

Such a festival was being held in a small coast village near the
Moulmein in Burma and the place was *en fête* in consequence. The
brightly coloured silks of the crowd as they gathered near the shore
in the cool of the evening while the sun was setting behind a bank of
gold and rosy clouds made a scene of brilliant colouring.

It was in this setting that the shrine, along with several others,
was launched with many blessings and prayers on the bosom of the
open sea. This shrine was seven feet high, built of wood and paper
and decorated with red and yellow flags. Inside the little temple was
an image of Buddha, about two feet high, and around this were
placed lighted candles and bowls of rice, fruit and money. The latter
amounted to over eleven rupees, nearly £1, mostly in very small
change, and was placed in a glass alms bowl. The whole was on a
wooden raft about ten feet square.

The wind at that season in those parts blows from the North East and so the little rafts were soon wafted out of sight of the watching Burmans. The little fleet was doubtless soon separated over the ocean as they were blown south across the Bay of Bengal.

Severe storms and high winds are common in October and the sea is seldom smooth. Cyclones too are fairly common at hat rime and doubtless most of the fragile craft did not long survive the elements and, becoming waterlogged, sank. But the one I write of braved the storm day and night for three months and eventually, in January it neared land again and was beached on the sandy shores of a beautiful wooded island of the Middle Andaman.

Our little raft had left from a land of laughter and sunshine and found its way to those islands, too often the scene of pain and despair. Other than the rapidly dying out race of Andamanese aboriginals the inhabitants of the islands were guests of the Indian Government, banished there for the remainder of their natural lives, or for a shorter period should the judge see fit. But, besides the several thousands of convicts, there were several hundreds of free coolies who were recruited in India and Burma to work in the large forest camps of the Andaman Islands. Large consignments of timber were exported to India or elsewhere throughout the world from these inlands. It was near one of these forest camps that our shrine landed.

Early one morning some of the Burman coolies at Middle Andaman, and curiously enough two of them were from the very village from which the shrine had been dispatched, were walking along the shore to work in the forest when they sighted the red pagoda as it danced on the waves breaking gently on the shore, the sight filled them with joy for it seemed like a breath from their beloved home land; and running out they carried it triumphantly ashore.

The arrival of the floating shrine was taken as being a direct message from the Spirits and homage was done to it at once. On being carried inland to the camp it was greeted with delight by all the Burmans and was soon erected as a shrine. Among things found intact in the little pagoda was a message in a sealed bottle asking the finder to send word of its arrival; this was done immediately, the local Headman arranging for a telegram to be sent.

Doubtless the devout Burman who set the little shrine adrift felt rewarded for his act and it certainly was the means of considerable comfort to hundreds of his fellow countrymen who, when their hard day's work was done, came to meditate and pray at that peaceful spot in the Andaman forests.

Appendix 5
A Trip to the Nicobars
by Elizabeth Lowis
The Times of India
6 June 1920

If you cannot have a 'wet sheet and a flowing sail' perhaps the next best thing for the ocean traveller in the tropics, is a comfortably appointed and steady-going ship.

It was on R.I.M.S. *Dalhousie* that we found ourselves one brilliant morning early in April. The harbour of Port Blair on such a morning is bathed in sunshine, a gentle north east wind keeping the temperature wonderfully cool. The surrounding islands, though still emerald green where perennial forests grow, yet show brown parts where the April sun has burnt the grass on the slopes. The sea sparkles like cut sapphires around us. It is our fine weather season and except for the ripples caused by the breeze, there is a perfectly calm sea as the anchor is weighed and we steam quietly out of the harbour and down the coast of South Andaman.

Low lying forest clad hills sloping up from broad stretches of yellow sand, many of them fringed with coconut palms form the coast line for miles around these parts.

We are bound first for South Sentinel, an outlying island of the Andaman group. It is seldom visited and has no human inhabitants, unlike North Sentinel on which the unfriendly little Jarawa Anadamanese still hold their own. South Sentinel measures barely a mile in length or breadth.

It is the breeding ground of turtle and the home of large and rare Robber crab. It lies due south and after about six hours going we find ourselves lying off the little island.

There is the usual coral reef around and the surf even in this weather is breaking in white foam against the rocks at one end of the island.

These waters are only partly surveyed and it is no easy job for the ships commander to find an anchorage. We are fortunate in having a venerated and intrepid captain and very soon we are safely anchored about a hundred yards from the shore. In less than ten minutes we are in a ship's boat and rowing for the beach. The sea is crystal clear, and the boat seems almost resting on the top of the great brilliant coloured, coral rocks; but we get safely over, and land high and dry in a sheltered corner of the beach; the lascars and ships officers all jumping out to pull the boat up the last few yards on the sand.

Here we scatter going our several ways to explore the island. Two of the party have their guns, and make off after pigeon, into the dense jungle growth which covers the island.

Very soon some of the Burmans have got on the track of a large iguana lizard. They are slow going gentle creatures, but are alarming in appearance, and look like small crocodiles as they shuffle through the undergrowth. The men managed to catch two after a short chase. Their skins are very fine and soon Lamba, our Burman orderly, (who always accompanies us on these sort of expeditions as he is useful and a sportsman), has a skin clearly stripped and ready to take on board.

Some of the party make for the headland where the rocks jut out under the wood, and as they looked down into the wonderfully clear sea, a huge shark is seen lying basking in the sunshine close in shore against a ledge of rock. This rather spoils the prospects of the bathers who are looking forward to a swim. Close by the sharks there are several turtles swimming about; their whole bodies clearly visible in that water. Every now and then they raise their heads to breath, but do not go far out and are evidently just putting in time till the invaders have left the island.

As we walk along the beach, there are large scooped out places in the sand and the marks of turtle are clearly visible; in these hollows many bits of the soft, sun-dried white egg shells are to be seen and if we came three weeks earlier we should have found these turtle homes full of eggs, or very young turtles, as I have seen them once previously.

A very fine green hackled pigeon was shot by Lieut. B of the ship. It is a beautiful large bird with wonderful metallic green feathers, and is only found in these islands.

So far we have failed to find a Robber crab; but later on when some of us were enjoying a cautious bathe in the warm sea, in spite of the shark, R appeared in the distance carrying one of these extraordinary creatures. He had met this one stalking through the jungle.

This crab's peculiarity is that it measures about 2½ feet across. He had enormous claws. The two front ones look capable of awful destruction, one being larger than the other. It is believed to climb the palm trees and nip off the nuts which it eats on the ground. It is many years since one of these specimens has been secured, and they do not usually live long in captivity, but we have hopes that this one may live in comfort, though a prisoner, as he seems to enjoy his meals of fruit, rejecting the meals of fish or meat we try and tempt him with. His shell is a mottled pink and green colour and his claws are a deep red. It is of much less ferocious disposition than the small crabs and seldom raises its claws as those do when provoked.

By this time the sun is sinking behind the island and as we had to get away before dark, we were soon rowing back to the ship with our queer property and no sooner on board than we are on the move again heading still further south for Car Nicobar.

Here we arrive early morning. Sawi Bay, Car Nicobar is a wide stretch of sand, about a mile in length, the sand of a rare deep golden colour which with luxurious green and brown of jungle and rocks make a beautiful picture of vivid colouring.

Here the anchor is barely down before several little Nicobarese canoes with picturesque outriggers are paddling out from the shore to greet our arrival and soon several of the natives are aboard. They are a strongly made cheery lot. One of our party is Mr H, the British agent at Car Nicobar, a man much respected by the local community. His is no light task as he has to keep the peace between the many Indian traders (who frequent these islands trading for coconuts), and the Aborigines.

The latter's wealth consists entirely of these coconuts. The traders bring cloth and oil and a variety of things for which they get large stocks of nuts to take back in their sailing ships, to India or the Straits. There is a mission station here also though at present no man can be spared to shepherd the little flock of Christians and a medical man of zeal and enthusiasm is sorely needed to help these simple and very attractive folk. At present an Indian catechist's widow does her best to keep the few Christian girls together, and some of our party went and heard them read and sing in the school house. Nicobarese has no written language, but parts of the New Testament has been translated and written down in Roman script and this some of the girls read easily, several of the boys have been sent to school in Burma at various times and four of these were fighting for Britain in the late war and did well in their various jobs. After a visit to the school and the little wooden church, where Mrs Solomon plays the organ with one finger to accompany the hymns on Sunday, we go on to Mr H's bungalow where several traders are already awaiting him with questions as to their licenses to trade and other matters. Later we walk along the road through the coconut plantation to the beach on the other side of the island. Here are the large communal huts, which every inhabited island possesses for its community. There is the large birth hut where we look in cautiously and see three women with their tiny babies. Further along the beach is the death hut. Here we find a poor old woman dying of cancer of the jaw, bought on, the ships doctor says by constant betel nut chewing. She is the wife of old Uffundi, the headman who came to welcome us. Like all the village head men of these islands, on arrival of the Government ship, he dons a suit of khaki drill given them by a grateful Government, and a large soft hat to show rank. His friends around who wear the scantiest attire, look much more appropriately clad, for the thermo-meter in these parts seldom falls below 80 but Uffundi is proud of his clothes. He had begged R to go and see his wife and it was sad to feel that we were powerless to help him. The old couple are very attached Mr H tells us and it is pitiful to see his concern for his poor wife. Uffundi comes on board with us later and gets the usual presents of sugar, tea and tobacco and goes off satisfied to keep his sad vigil again. After lunch on board we enjoy a bathe in the huge surf on the golden beach before we weigh anchor and are off south once more.

We are now going to Great Nicobar and as we reach that island and steam along the coast we notice the higher hills, and much more rugged aspect of the scenery. It might be the West coast of Scotland or Ireland. Here; last autumn, a steamer lost her way, and struck the coast when on her voyage from Singapore to Madras. As we get near her we can see that she is hard on a rock close to the shore, but the ship is apparently unbroken. No lives were lost, for a passing steamer had been summoned by wireless. Some Chinese junks had been here before us and the decks were strewn with their leavings, and all the fittings had been torn off; books clothes, papers and rubbish of all sorts have been strewn about the deck, making the deserted ship a sad sight. Probably in a few weeks' time when the south west monsoon sets in the poor derelict will be knocked to pieces on the rocks where she now lies on an even keel.

R. brings me as a memento, a menu of the last dinner on board that ill-fated ship. The Captain and all of us are glad to be off from such a scene of desolation and before night falls we are anchored in Galatea Bay, the most southerly point of the Nicobar Islands.

Next morning early we turned north and homewards again, and are soon looking for an anchorage where the charts only show marked, 'Numerous reefs and shoals reported'. We are not to be put off all the same, and are pleasantly surprised to find deep water to within a couple of miles of the shore off Kanalla. Here the surf breaking on the beach is so great that a white mist of foam spray hangs thick along the coast line. Two canoes come off immediately with their weird crews, occupants of the little brown-thatched huts we can see against the jungle.

We go off this time in the ship's steam cutter, taking the head man with us as guide. His head is an odd shape and he wears a chief's suit of Khaki drill and an old top hat, and as he stands up in the cutter beside the First Officer who is steering us through the intricate reefs. He directs us into a quiet bay where on both sides up and down the coast can be seen those wonderful huge breakers as they swell in mountainous form towards the reef where they break in great white waves and throw the spray far up so that it is seen for miles around.

The inhabitants here have not seen Englishmen for many years and few of them have ever seen English woman before and are duly interested. The rare megapod is known to breed here and soon we are following a native through the jungle where the tree ferns and tropical growth of all sorts, are even more noticeable than in the other places we have visited. As we emerge from the forest, on the further shore and at the edge of the beach is the great mound of sand which the megapods in this vicinity use as a nursery. They lay their eggs here buried deep in the sand, and leave them to hatch and the little ones forage for themselves when they appear. The megapod is a small brown bird in shape like a guinea fowl. It differs very slightly from the Australian bush turkey. Its chief peculiarity besides the sandy incubator is the size of the egg it lays. The bird is the size of a small guinea fowl and lays an egg the size of an extra large turkey's egg of a smooth texture and of a light brown colour. The small megapod is hatched fully fledged and able to fight its way out of the sandy mound and fly off on its own account.

The natives in these parts use cross bows of wood for shooting birds. Some of these and some genuine 'scare devils' were bought from Nicobarese here. These latter form the only approach to religion that these people have in their lives. They live in dread of evil spirits, and their huts are decorated inside especially near the opening, with roughly painted birds and men being the principal models used. Outside their villages and on the sea shore are tall bamboos decorated at intervals with bunches of grass, these are put here for the same purpose, that is to say to scare away evil spirits.

In the more northern islands it is difficult to get a genuine devil-scarer nowadays, the natives there being even suspected for making them for trade, but in Great Nicobar the genuine articles abound.

From this place we put off to the ship again in a long narrow Nicobarese canoe with outrigger, with barely room to sit or put your feet, but far the safest mode of conveyance over coral reefs. The natives use small wooden paddles, and are very clever in manipulating them over the surf.

Our destination was Chowra Island. Here the natives have a reputation for incivility and independence. They are feared by the inhabitants of the other islands for their supposed control of the evil spirits. Chowra is a very small island with a comparatively large population and very few coconuts and consequently no trade. Necessity being the mother of invention, the inhabitants have somehow acquired the monopoly of the trade in cooking pots; all pots used throughout the islands must be made in Chowra. This had been going on for centuries as is evidenced by the fact that the supplies of clay on the island have long ago been worked out, and for many years they have had to draw their supplies of clay from Teressa Island, about ten miles distant by sea. No Nicobarese in any of the other islands dare to make a cooking pot for himself, and they have to undergo long voyages sometimes forty or fifty miles in their frail craft to obtain their annual supply of pots. These voyages are made in the calm weeks during March and April, but even so it occasionally happens that canoes are lost on the voyages and the period is an anxious one on the islands situated furthest from Chowra.

We were agreeably surprised to find the natives as pleasant as they appeared. Chowra village consists of a long straggling line of huts more inland than is usually the case, and much more tidily kept. On the wooden platforms below the huts we found women in the act of finishing off large earthen vessels really for firing. They only used their hands and bits of pointed and smooth wood for fashioning the pots.

Here one of our party took a fancy to a beautifully modelled toy canoe, which he paid for with a shirt, and carried off in triumph. It is destined to sail in the Round Pond, and is sure to cause a flutter in the racing there.

The beach at Chowra was strewn with bits of sponge of a very brittle variety.

As we put off to the ship once more, two little white specks could be seen on the distant horizon, and the Chowra men seemed in great spirits over the fact. The specks proved to be sails of canoes laden with natives coming from Car Nicobar to trade for pots.

As we boarded the ship again we were sorry to think we were leaving those beautiful islands with their happy and contented inhabitants who, however much the outside world may fight and struggle, still continue to lead their sleepy lives where nature supplies all their wants.

Next day we anchored in Port Blair harbour, having had a most interesting and delightful trip in perfect weather.

The Andaman Islands : A Family Connection
by Mrs L.V. Deane (née Mary Lowis)
BBC Radio
26 January 1969

When one is asked 'Where were you born?' a slight stir is caused by the reply 'The Andaman Islands'. Yet no less than four generations of my family were born or served in that lovely group of islands in the Indian Ocean.

My first memory of the Andamans is being carried off the little steamship *Bess* (called after my mother) at the age of five to live for two perfect childhood years, with my parents, in their breezy hillside house, overlooking the dazzling harbour between the islands of Aberdeen and Ross.

My father was then deputy commissioner of the Andamans, and his duties involved him in endless cruises to the outlying islands, with his menage of my mother, my brother, myself, our English governess, our dog and a pet mongoose. We drifted delightedly about the sunlit sea, undaunted by the occasional shower of

'The little steamship *Bess*' was used for 'endless cruises to the outlying islands'.

John and Mary Lowis with Andaman islander children and a young turtle (1913).

poisoned arrows, which greeted us from the independent indigenous, little Andamanese pygmies in their jungle. But if they showed any sign of welcome, we all climbed with dignity from our craft, and made the greatest friends with the tiny shining creatures, unclothed but for their pretty beads. The friendship for us children was finally cemented when they mounted us on enormous turtles, which we ponderously raced up and down the beach. Then, if we were thirsty, a small boy would dart up a palm tree, to cut and throw down a coconut, and then came the bliss of that ice cold milk drunk straight from the shell.

At home on the mainland our day used to start with gallops about the island on great police-guard horses, attended by great police-guard Sikhs who occasionally caught us as we bounced from our huge mounts, and tossed us back into the saddle unharmed.

We never suffered from any sense of insecurity or fear, though surrounded and served by convicted murderers day and night. They seemed to dote upon us and spent endless hours devising exquisite toys for us from palm leaves and shells. Looking back, in fact, this seems to have been one of the most tranquil, carefree and safe periods of my life.

Yet the lurking rumours of violence were familiar to us all. The murdered viceroy, Lord Mayo; my poor murdered cousin, Lady d'Oyley, who scolded her water-carrier just once too often and was hacked to death in her bath; even my own near-drowning at Corbyns Cove when I was dragged from my father's shoulders by a towering wave and disappeared into the boiling sea, only to be rescued by my very long hair which served as a rope to heave me back to safety: these incidents never cast a shadow on our lives, though in 1915, at the beginning of the war, I do remember the threat of the German warship the *Emden* which had orders to establish a German harbour in the neighbouring Nicobar Islands, and at one point turned tail and fled after a Nicobarese woman, clad only in a top hat hoisted the Union Jack. (The total population of the Nicobar Islands is only a few hundred people.)

Shortly after this, I left the Andaman Islands to go to school in England, never thinking to return, but, astonishingly I did return as a young bride, when my husband was posted to this remote place in 1930 as an assistant commissioner. My second chapter merges now into the first, all shining sea, and sun and gentle winds.

Again I lived in high, bright, spacious rooms, but again, the giant experience comes to mind of a huge barracuda at the end of a fishing-line which all but dragged me into the sea had I not been clutched and held by my husband, as we heaved a great fifty pound fish on to the deck of the ship.

It was there on Ross Island that both our children were born in the early thirties on that small island where my great uncle Sir George had gone to live in the 1890s, where my own mother had served him as hostess as a girl, where she met my father and married him in 1900 and where I was born and spent my childhood.

And so, our sad sailing away, in 1934, bedecked with gorgeous fragrant garlands, seemed the end of not two but only one, happy chapter in my life in the little paradise called Port Blair.

Illustrations

Page 108   Above: Watching cricket at the Ross Island Club. Date unknown. Photo: Lawley family archive.

Page 108   Below: Picnic. Bessie Lowis sits centre, facing away. Location and date unknown. Photo: Lawley family archive.

Page 110   Reggie and Bessie Lowis. Location and date unknown. Photo: Lawley family archive.

Page 111   Elizabeth and Janet Lowis. Location and date unknown. Photo: Lawley family archive.

Page 117   Reginald Lowis with a group of Andaman islanders, photographed by Sir Henry Seton-Karr during the 1911 census. Image 400 113265, Seton-Karr Collection. Courtesy: The Royal Anthropological Institute of Great Britain and Ireland.

Page 119   Andaman tribesmen in dug-out canoes. Location and date unknown. Photo: Lawley family archive.

Page 120   Andaman tribesmen fishing with spears. Location and date unknown. Photo: Lawley family archive.

Page 126   John and Mary Lowis holding hands with Andaman Island children, 1913. Location unknown. Photo: Lawley family archive.

Page 185   The *Bess* steamship, used for census-taking and other official duties. Named after Bessie Lowis. Location and date unknown. Photo: Lawley family archive.

Page 186   John and Mary Lowis with Andaman Islands children and a young turtle (1913).